D1179829

JAZZ:
A PEOPLE'S MUSIC

A Da Capo Press Reprint Series

THE ROOTS OF JAZZ

JAZZ:
A PEOPLE'S MUSIC

BY
SIDNEY FINKELSTEIN

DA CAPO PRESS • NEW YORK • 1975

Library of Congress Cataloging in Publication Data

Finkelstein, Sidney Walter, 1909-1974.
    Jazz, a people's music.

    (The Roots of jazz)
    Reprint of the 1st ed., 1948, published by Citadel
Press, New York.
    Includes discographies and index.
    1. Jazz music. 2. Jazz music—Discography.
I. Title.
ML3561.J3F5   1975   785.4'2'0973   74-23386
ISBN 0-306-70659-8

This Da Capo Press edition of *Jazz* is an unabridged republication
of the first edition published in New York in 1948. It is reprinted
with the permission of The Citadel Press.

Published by Da Capo Press, Inc.
A Subsidiary of Plenum Publishing Corporation
227 West 17th Street, New York, N.Y. 10011

Manufactured in the United States of America

JAZZ
A PEOPLE'S MUSIC

SIDNEY FINKELSTEIN

ILLUSTRATED BY JULES HALFANT

THE CITADEL PRESS, NEW YORK

COPYRIGHT 1948
The Citadel Press

PRINTED IN THE UNITED STATES OF AMERICA
BY J. J. LITTLE & IVES COMPANY, NEW YORK

This year has seen the birth of the state of Israel. It is to the people of the new nation that this book is dedicated knowing that they, fighting for independence, will welcome this story of another people's struggle for freedom, and their creation of a culture.

C O N T E N T S

CHAPTER 7

THE FUTURE OF JAZZ

The Failure of Jazz Composition . . . Stravinsky and Others . . . Modern Music and Folk Language . . . Jazz and Jim Crow . . . New Forms for Jazz . . . A People's Theatre . . .

PREFACE

People who create jazz generally don't write about it, and jazz records have a way of being remembered after theories about them are long forgotten. If there were no art, there would be no books about it. Writers are often only faintly aware of realities which the jazz musician knows but cannot describe.

Yet there is a legitimate task for the writer on jazz, as on any art. It is to bring understanding of the art to a greater number of people, and also to put the art itself into a perspective which the individual creator himself may not see.

This book attempts to tackle a problem which has been left unsolved ever since the beginning of jazz history. It is to place jazz as part of world music. The artificial distinction between "classical" and "popular," "highbrow" and "low brow," is ready for the ashcan. Jazz is the most important single body of music yet produced in America. But on the other hand, jazz is not helped by the exaggerated claims of some of its admirers, who consider it the "music of the future," and find no other music worth knowing. Jazz must be studied for both its achievements and limitations. The first is necessary in order to break down the snobbery which still keeps jazz from being properly respected as a great music. The second is necessary in order to reveal the contradictions that still beset jazz, and to chart the road that it still has to travel. For jazz has a future as well as a past, and its surprises are by no means limited to its past history.

There exists a considerable literature about jazz, to all of which this book is greatly indebted. The first writing about jazz consisted of the listing of thousands of records, which had been issued mainly for a Negro public by companies that had no idea of their musical value. The names of the musicians who took part on these recordings were unearthed, and slowly a picture was formed of the outstanding men who had brought a new music into being. This collection of data was a magnificent piece of collective scholarship, although never called by that highfaluting name, and done by men whose main guide was their love for the music and keenness of ear. It required, moreover, close collaboration between the collectors and the musicians themselves. Critics abroad as well as at home took part in this research, and the classic compilation of record data is Charles Delaunay's "Hot Discography," although it is now rivaled by Orrin Blackstone's "Index to Jazz."

The French critic, Hugues Panassie, wrote the first analytic study of jazz to be widely read in America. Translated in 1936, as "Hot Jazz," it provided the beginning student and collector with a guide to the bewildering wealth of material, and also gave the veteran collector many ideas to argue over. Today its theories no longer stand up. They were from the start attempts to find analytic words for what were only subjective impressions. Its great qualities, which still carry through today, were its genuine enthusiasm for the music, its willingness to point out some works as better than others, the fine ear for music of genuine stature that its author displayed.

"Jazzmen," a collective historical study edited by Frederick Ramsey, Jr., and Charles Edward Smith, appeared in 1939, and carried the understanding of jazz a step forward. In this book, unlike Panassie's, jazz appeared as the creation of an entire people more than of a few representative musicians. The authors were able

to recreate in words a musical life, mainly of New Orleans, which was only faintly represented on records.
Today there seems in the book to be too poetic a nostalgia
thrown about the life of the Negro people in the South,
and it is now apparent that the movement of the music
North was not the great tragedy it appeared to be to the
writers. This movement was a necessary forward step for
jazz. But the book is still the best documentary history of
the early days of jazz.

Winthrop Sargeant's "Jazz, Hot and Hybrid," appearing in 1938, brought to jazz the scrutiny of a professional music critic. Its weakness was that it tried to
generalize, from a few selected records, some characteristics that were common to all. The author had no knowledge of the variety of moods and forms in the music, its
origins and constantly changing content. Its study, however, of the chord structures, scale systems and rhythmic
patterns of jazz were an improvement on Panassie's definition of "hot style," and still have value today.

Panassie's second book, "The Real Jazz," published
in 1942, showed little advance over his first. In correcting
the overemphasis of his first book on the work of the
white musicians in Chicago, and evaluating the great
achievements of the early Negro musicians, he fell into
the error common among European critics of making a
folk and a people's art synonymous with the "primitive."
Thus he says, "In music, primitive man has generally
greater talent than civilized man," a foolish statement

whether referring to jazz or to Beethoven. His tastes, so far as the progress of jazz was concerned, remained confined to the boundaries of ten years before, missing the boat on Basie and Lester Young.

"The Jazz Record Book," by Charles Edward Smith assisted by Frederick Ramsey, Jr., Charles Payne Rogers and William Russell, also appeared in 1942. This book carried the approach of "Jazzmen" into record analysis. Its first 125 pages are an excellent compact history of the rise of jazz, thankfully lacking in primitivistic theories. The record criticisms are sharp and perceptive. The weakness of the book was that the authors limited themselves to the records actually in print at the time. Had the writers ignored the vagaries of record companies, and done what they can do so well—evaluate the main body of the recorded literature of New Orleans jazz and the blues—they would have expended less space on music they didn't really like and provided a guide to collectors, students and record companies that would stand up today.

Robert Goffin's "Jazz: From the Congo to the Metropolitan," his second book but the first to appear in English, was published in 1944. He carried further the study of the background of jazz, making some interesting points about the reappearance of old French folk songs in jazz. He failed to develop this point further, however, falling instead into the "African," "primitive" and "subconscious" theories of jazz. He looked on jazz almost as if it were another kind of esthetic experiment such as took place in Paris in the 1920's, one with dada, surrealism and automatic writing. He also gave jazz the left-handed compliment of lavishing praise upon it, and then saying that "music has no need of the intelligence." The truth is that all art, and jazz is no exception, grows out of man's ability to think as well as to feel.

"Shining Trumpets," by Rudi Blesh, which appeared in 1946, carried the "folk," "primitive" and "African" theory of jazz to its furthest extreme. Its most worthwhile quality was that it carried the exploration of the roots of jazz back into the blues and spirituals of the past century. But this music, while most important to jazz, is not identical with jazz. And in taking the further leap into Africa, seeing only similarities and no differences, Blesh transformed what might have been a valuable theory of the continuity of musical development into a dogmatic and abstract definition of jazz, which was a barrier to the understanding of the music and of the people who made it. Instead of seeing that jazz and American folk music has been continually changing, to Blesh there was no change of importance up to the 1920's, and then a vast change which causes him to call all new jazz produced since, no matter how earnest its efforts to express new feelings and develop new techniques, a "commercial conspiracy."

Theories concerning races and inheritance of "racial characteristics" are advanced in the name of science, although such theories have been discredited by most scientists. The attitude towards the Negro people is one of great sympathy, but deficient in understanding. The suffering of the Negro people was not so passive as he describes it, and the music was not so escapist. The Negro people struggled in the most realistic way against slavery, through revolts, the Underground Railroad, and their heroic role in the Civil War. They struggled in the most realistic way against all forms of discrimination and Jim Crowism that followed the Civil War. The music was a weapon in these struggles, and had the people not had the vitality to fight realistically for freedom, they would not have had the vitality to create this great music. As in the case of other similar theorists, the backward-looking approach to the music is bolstered by an attack on "civilized" music. Jazz, to Blesh, is sheer improvisation, and "with it Western music as we know it disappears and its composers, too."

The present book is aimed at breaking down barriers. There is first the barrier between jazz and concert music, each considering itself a world apart, although each suffers from the lack of qualities that the other possesses. There is, as well, the narrow partisanship that has grown up within jazz itself, seen for example in the cultist atmosphere that has grown about both bebop and the New Orleans revival. This seeking in music for a fad is a sign of immaturity among jazz followers. People come before music. They fashion music to fit their needs, and discard it when they no longer need it. They have too many different needs of heart and mind to be satisfied by a single approach to musical form. Bebop has remarkable qualities, and the New Orleans revival reminds us of other beauties which have been lost. Neither supplies either musicians or audience with all that they have a right to ask of the art of music.

There is a partisanship needed today. It is a partisanship against the insincerity, the callous imitation and plagiarism of musical ideas, the misuse and destruction of human genius, that infest both the world of popular music and the concert world. The divisions that exist in both the popular and the concert musical world are only a sign of the fact that the musician of today does not have the opportunity to work out his problems in the most rational and productive manner. What we need to fight for is the conditions under which we can begin to solve these problems in the most real and practical way. This, as I will try to show, is a problem of American life as well as of American music.

The illustrative lists that follow the chapters dealing with the many styles and developments of jazz consist of records which at this writing are available for purchase. In addition I have tried to indicate the nature of the most important material now out of print, which should be made available again for study.

I am indebted to Irving Ravinsky, George Avakian, Alfred Lion, Grant Adams and Ross Russell for the opportunity to hear many records which I did not have.

SIDNEY FINKELSTEIN

CHAPTER ONE

THE PLACE OF JAZZ
IN MUSIC HISTORY

There are not two worlds of music, but only one. Within this one world there are many different kinds of music. The division however, between "classical" and "popular," "highbrow" and "lowbrow," has no meaning whatsoever as a test of quality. Jazz is not simply a great "popular" music but a great music.

9

The seeming division we find today between the "classical" and "popular" is a recent development in the art. Great composers like Bach, Handel, Purcell, Mozart, Schubert and Verdi wrote songs and dances, as well as opera, concerto, cantata, symphony and oratorio. They were delighted when their music was taken up and sung or danced to by people in the streets. A Schubert symphony is a more massive and admirable achievement than a Schubert song, but a Schubert song is infinitely more alive than a four-movement symphony or a three hour opera by some composer who is now forgotten because he had nothing to say.

Sheer size or nobility of intentions has nothing to do with the value of a work of music. Good music asserts the presence within it of a living, thinking and feeling human being, exploring the world about him. Bad music attempts to satisfy the needs of the present by finding formulas in the past. It dilutes and reshuffles past music to give a superficial appearance of novelty. Starting with this division, we may find subdivisions. Within good music, there are some works which deal with more complicated human and emotional problems than others. Within bad music, there are some composers who are more competent at their craft than others, and so offer hope that they may yet come to life. But the division between good and bad, living and mechanical, is fundamental.

In our own time, as in the past, the distinction between creative and mechanically concocted music cuts across the artificial distinction between "classical" and "popular." A symphonic work may represent years of study by the composer of the great music of the past. It may require ninety first-class instrumentalists and take an hour for its performance. Yet if there is no original thought and feeling in it, no touch of the strangeness and beauty which comes when an artist has reacted to life as well as to art, it remains bad music. A jazz work may be put together by sheer improvisation, for the most immediate use of dance or song. It may take only three minutes to perform, and be created by musicians with little knowledge of the history or elaborated techniques of musical production. If it has this quality of emotional and human truth, the combination of strangeness and familiarity which arises only when musical notes take on a pattern of living human experience, it is good music.

The term jazz includes an enormous amount of musical production. Much of it is bad music, just as the greater part of the composed music pouring from our conservatories is bad music. Yet there is a golden vein in jazz of genuine music, produced by men who regard a musical instrument as an extension of their hand, voice and mind, who regard music as a language with which they speak to their fellow human beings. Added up, this genuine creation within jazz is an imposing production, the most important and lasting body of music yet produced in the United States. It is for this music, as for our handful of worthwhile symphonic, chamber music and operatic works, that our age will be respected in the future. And it will make no difference to later times that this great body of jazz was produced mainly by unlettered musicians, and by the most exploited of people among us, except as an interesting and revealing sidelight into the contradictions of musical culture in our times.

Why has this contradiction grown up in our times between the "classical" and the "popular"? The difference is not one of complexity as against simplicity. The man who listens to creative jazz, whether "New Orleans" or bebop, is hearing as unstandardized a set of musical scales and combinations of scales, as is he who listens to Copland or Ives. To pick apart the interplay of two melodic lines, and the rhythmic pattern which both supports and plays against them, in a jazz work, is as demanding on the listener as to follow the structure of a Bach fugue. To discover that the clarinet on a pre-electrical recording is being played by Johnny Dodds or Buster Bailey is as fine a piece of musicology as to place the origin and period of an anonymous musical manuscript.

The artificial distinction between "classical" and "popular" has been forced upon our times by the circumstance that the production of both "classical" and "popular" music in our time has become a matter for financial investment instead of an art. Both the giving of classical concerts and the production of popular music have become great business enterprises, representing capital which must be protected by establishing a standardized commodity.

The result is that our concert music has become predominantly "classical," meaning of the past. If we were to judge from the symphonic, solo concert and operatic programs given in America during the past two or three decades, we would conclude that the art of music was one produced by dead men; that music was not an art in which the listeners expected a communication from a living contemporary.

This is not pointed out in order to minimize the greatness of men like Bach, Beethoven and Schubert, or the importance of knowing their work. These composers were, however, living human beings when they wrote their music, addressing in the most exciting way whatever people they could reach of their own times. To base our listening experiences predominantly on works of the distant past is like looking to history not for help in understanding today, and solving our own problems, but for a romantic escape to a fabulous golden age.

Music was meant to sound, in the past, not sweet but exciting. When we contrast the conflicts which great music aroused in the past, among its hearers, to its apparently innocuous sweetness today, it is sometimes taken as a sign that we have learned how to listen to this music. The truth is the opposite. We have learned how not to listen. All good music should sound fresh, exciting, daring, since it is the work of a man with a new human experience to communicate, who uses the language of his art a little differently from anyone before him.

The badness of a great deal of our contemporary concert musical composition, is due to the fact that many composers, aware that our concert music is predominantly that of "dead men," decide to compose like dead men. The common term for this procedure is academicism. Such works of disguised imitation are highly acceptable to promoters, for they fit easily into the common methods of performance, make small demands on mind or technique, challenge no prejudice or hidebound ways of thinking. They quickly die, for they were lifeless to start with; but are replaced by new works cut to the same model.

The bad "popular" music that is produced in such quality is bad for similar reasons. Its low level does not come from any desire to fit music to the needs of the people. The people, whenever they have produced their own music, reached high quality. The reason is that this mis-termed "popular" music is likewise a music of "dead men." Most of it is a travesty of the symphonic, operatic music and light opera of the past century; a pale imitation of a familiar melody given a text-book harmony and an instrumentation taken from a Chaikovsky overture or a Mendelssohn concerto. When Freddy Martin offers the Grieg concerto "for dancing," he is only doing more openly what has been done thousands of times before in more disguised form.

It is no accident that the composer of honest, creative jazz music, and the composer of honest, creative concert music, find themselves in parallel difficulties, although they produce an entirely different-sounding kind of music. Both are faced with powerful rivals. And these rivals do not depend for success on the power of the music they offer. Their strength is the power of money, of a financial network controlling the means of production and distribution of music, whether popular or concert hall.

Creative jazz has been violently attacked. It is called "primitive," "barbaric." The fact that it was produced mainly by the Negro people of America has been held against it. The fact that it found a home sometimes in brothels or speakeasies, that in its atmosphere and communication it reflects the miserable conditions of life forced upon the Negro people, has also been held against it. Unfortunately many of its defenders likewise misinterpret it. Some almost gloat in its gin-mill or brothel local color, as if they were basic to the music instead of accidental, with no relation whatsoever to the essential quality of the music except a destructive one. They praise it as "primitive," calling it an "African" or "Afro-American" music, whose wonderful qualities only prove that "intelligence" and "civilization" are harmful to music; certainly a lefthanded compliment to the people

who gave us these riches. They praise it because it needs no great technical command of an instrument or the art of writing music, and spin theories that greater technique and knowledge are harmful to "real" jazz, as if the music was created by the limited technique instead of by people who created out of whatever resources they had. They praise it as a complete break with all previous music, or all "Western" music.

Such defenses, although well meant, do almost as much harm as the attacks. The truth is that although jazz is in some ways a wholly new music, in other and very important ways it is not a new music at all. There has been no music exactly like it known to scholars. But at the same time part of its importance is that it charts for us an entire blank area of the past of music history.

Present day historical research indicates that the music which forms the basis for histories of the art, the music written down, is only a fraction of the vast amount of music that people actually played, sang and heard in past centuries. Each age had its "unwritten" as well as its written music. We know of this unwritten music from documentary description. Paul Henry Lang, for example, in his "Music in Western Civilization," quotes a fifteenth century scholastic commentator, Adam of Fulda, as one who "complained indignantly against the 'inordinate' influence exerted by the instrumentalists upon musical composition, and was appalled by the threatening possibility of the 'buffoons and minstrels becoming the composers of the future'." [1]

This attack upon the rough and boisterous music played by the common city people, and threatening to replace the fine-spun serenity of the cultivated church and aristocratic music of the time, sounds so much like the attacks upon jazz that we can guess the music was

[1] Paul Henry Lang, *Music in Western Civilization*, New York, W. W. Norton, 1941, p. 244.

very much the same. We also get a hint of the nature of this people's music of the past through the exciting impact it made upon every live and experimenting composer, the effect it had upon almost every change of musical style. To cite a few examples, there were the European religious composers who used folk songs so prolifically in their religious music; the Italian, French and English madrigal composers, who drew so richly upon the rough-hewn, many-voiced popular music of their time; Martin Luther, who created the hymnology for German protestantism by setting newly written prayers to folk and popular songs, many of these transformed songs becoming the favorite hymns of American protestantism; Padre Martini, Mozart's teacher, who advised all his students to go to folk music; Lully, Vivaldi, Haydn, Mozart, Schubert who drew so richly upon folk and popular dance.

Jazz is therefore, historically, a music of the greatest importance. Thanks to its appearing in an age of the phonograph record, it is the first "unwritten" music that can be studied and known. In the rich examples it gives us of a music flowering out of the most simple melodic and rhythmic patterns into the most varied and complex forms, the most subtle interweaving of melodic lines and creation of rhythmic-melodic structures, it gives us an insight into the entire growth and history of the art of music. It helps us to reconstruct what must have happened in centuries long ago when people also created

their own unwritten music, which proved to be so horri-
fying to some theoreticians and so exciting to fresh thinking composers.

Certainly jazz can be traced back to African music;
a point that has been made much of by some writers who,
hearing records of African drumming and chanting, see
a resemblance to jazz, and leap at a theory. By the same
process of reasoning, however, seeing only resemblances
and no differences, European music can likewise be
traced back to the ancient Gregorian chants, which themselves originated in Asiatic, Greek and Hebrew music.
Jazz is not African music, as anyone can tell who com-
pares Johnny Dodds' "Joe Turner Blues," Louis Armstrong's "Knocking a Jug" or Kid Ory's "High Society,"
to an African drum or vocal performance. Jazz is not
even "Afro-American," a term comparatively new and
popular among jazz theoreticians. To use such a hyphenated term implies that there are two Americas. If any
part of America should be thus hyphenated, however, all
should be. We are all either Afro-Americans, Anglo-
Americans, Irish-Americans, Jewish-Americans, Italian-
Americans, and so on.

Jazz is an American music, of such emotional sin-
cerity and power, of such vitality and human appeal, of
such fitness to people's needs that it has been accepted,
either in comparatively pure or diluted form, as the great
American popular music of song and dance. It has elements which can be traced back to Africa, but also ele-

ments which can be traced back to many other old cultures; to European hymn tunes, French folk songs, Spanish songs and dances, mountain songs and dances which were transplanted growths from Europe. And more than all of these origins put together, it is a fresh and new musical creation, telling us of the emotional and social life, the sadness, anger and vitality of the Negro people who were brought here as slaves, who through their labor created so great a part of American civilization and American culture.

The Negro people are in a sense a group within America, a nation within a nation. This has not come about, however, through their own choice or through any mystical "African" characteristics. It is the result of the fact that the Negro people, torn from many different old cultures, were forcibly pressed into slavery. After the abolition of slavery they were confined to the meanest occupations, denied education, freedom of movement and citizen rights, given lowest pay, segregated in ghettos.

The Negro people have constantly fought against these conditions, and who can say that this struggle was not part of the making of America itself? Along with their struggle against slavery was the role they played in the War of Independence, out of which came the abolition of the slave trade, and the much underestimated role they played in the war to preserve the Union, out of which came the abolition of slavery. The congresses in the Southern States in which the Negro people took part after the Civil War, either ignored or misinterpreted in most history books, show how genuinely democratic the South might have become, had it not been for the Ku Klux Klan, the removal of Federal troops, and the resulting transformation of the South into a colony of Northern industry and banker investment.

Bound together by their common economic life and struggle, the Negro people have built up a history, tradition and cultural life of their own, along with a growing sense of their own nationhood. In this cultural life we can find African roots, but this does not determine its character any more than we can say that American democracy is "French" because the Declaration of Independence took much of its thinking from the great French liberals of the eighteenth century. The culture of the Negro people in America takes its shape from the conditions of American life of which the life of the Negro people is a part. A land does not take its life and character from those who own its property, or who speak for it. A land is given its real life and character by those who live and labor on it. Just as American history, economic life and civilization are to a considerable extent the creation of the Negro people, so American culture is to a considerable extent a creation of the Negro people.

This contribution has become so much a part of the very texture of American life that it cannot be isolated, torn out, examined as a separate entity. It should not surprise us that the music created largely by the American Negro people, the spirituals, blues and jazz, have been so widely accepted and adopted by the entire American people as their own music. This is only a reflection, within our cultural life, of the truth that the struggle of the Negro people for the right to education, freedom of movement, and an adequate role in government itself, is an organic part of the struggle for the growth of American democracy.

Jazz is not a "primitive" music. This is a theory often expressed in contemporary writings about jazz; that it throws listeners as well as musicians into a "hypnotic trance," or springs directly from the "subconscious." The word "primitive" itself, of course, is much misused as referring to tribal man. Tribal man was a very great creator. It was out of tribal civilization that we got our basic languages of communication, spoken, musical and pictorial; that we got the first tools and attempts to explain and master nature. People are not "primitive." Societies may be, in that certain stages in the conquest of nature are necessary so that other stages can develop out of them. If tribal man had not struggled, with whatever forces at his command, continually to better his life and bend nature more to his needs, there would be no "advanced" civilization today. With minor exceptions, people that still seem to be "backward" today are such because they are forcibly prevented from advancing.

The fairly recent appreciation of the elaborate cultural life of tribal civilizations was a great step forward in breaking down the myths of "white" or "Caucasian" supremacy. Anthropologists discovered that each culture had its own values, some of which put the moral values of industrial civilization to shame. Many of the anthropologists stopped at this point. Each culture has its own "values," they said, and is to be judged only by these "values."

Such appreciation of the achievements of tribal civilization, however, can be turned to the most reactionary use. For there is progress in human life, progress in respect to greater knowledge of the world, greater mastery over nature, greater potentialities of production and of human beings living better and more freely. How little these potentialities are actually realized in terms of the masses of people in "civilized" countries is not within the province of this particular book. These advances and potentialities, however, cultural and industrial, are every people's ability and right.

The theory of the equality of cultures has been used to excuse colonial exploitation. If all cultures are equally good for themselves, why change? Needless to say, proponents of this theory show no rush to put on loincloths, but are content to "admire" other cultures from a comfortable perspective. And also, needless to say, those who use colonial peoples for the most backbreaking labor at meagre pay, find the preservation of old myths, customs, ways of life, most useful to them.

These theories, then, of the noble simplicity of the "primitive," are highly suspect, even when advanced in good faith. And they are equally inapplicable to jazz.

Jazz is often a music of great basic simplicity, and gripping rhythmic force. It is also, at the same time, a music of great subtlety. Many of its melodic phrases and rhythmic patterns derive from African chants. But African music, like all tribal music, tends to be wholly of a group, and to fuse the group into one compelling emotion and movement. Children's music, indeed, is of a similar nature. In jazz, however, more than in tribal music, we find this group and social character combined with individual creation and thought. It is a music of interplay between the individual mind and the group. It is no more of a tribal character than we at a dance today can be said to resemble dancers in a tribal festival. Like them, we move to the same rhythm and pattern; yet at the same time we make this pattern elastic, and vary it with our own individual imagination. And so, in this respect, combining a social character with individual thought and feeling, combining a basic beat and repeated melody with the most elastic interplay and variation, jazz is far closer to European folk music and to composed music in dance forms, than it is to African. Oddly enough, some of the music of the 'twenties, such as Stravinsky's "Sacre du Printemps" and "Histoire du Soldat," written out of disgust with war and post-war culture with a conscious urge to embrace the "primitive," resembles African drums in its beat much more than jazz does.

The "subconscious" theory is another one of those pretty but misleading formulations based on half-truths. Jazz is not a product of the intelligence alone. No art is. Jazz is a flow of emotion in music guided by the most conscious skill, taste, artistry and intelligence. This is the character of the work of a Johnny Dodds, King Oliver, Louis Armstrong, "Jelly-Roll" Morton, Bessie Smith, Duke Ellington and Lester Young. It is often, however, independent and impolite, which is another matter entirely.

Neither is jazz wholly "improvised," nor at its best solely when created by musicians who can't read notes. The process of improvisation is central to jazz, but not so drastically different from the processes that go on in the mind of a composer who writes music; and the writing of music has had an important place in the history of jazz. Similarly the feeling of jazz musicians that they have a right to know and be able to master the full art of music as it exists today is a progressive step. Such musicians rightly suspect any attempt to limit them to what are real or fancied "folk" practises, no matter what the expressions of admiration of the old music that accompanies such limitations, as a subtle form of Jim-Crow. Jazz has had its history and constant change. At each period of its development, it produced a very great music. And each of these musical developments was created by

the jazz musician, predominantly Negro, when it answered to his needs. It was dropped or changed by him
when he felt new needs, and met new problems that
called for a different music. Anguished outcries rose from
those who had painfully learned to like the abandoned
music and were expressed in the most elaborate theo-
retical formulations. It is true that with each step forward
values were lost as well as gained. But the process of
change, development, exploration of new materials and
new emotions, is basic to jazz as it is to all living music.

If jazz is not to be defined as "African," or "Afro-
American," or "primitive," or "unconscious," or sheer
"improvisation," then why is it so different from what
passes for serious or composed music in our times? What
is its special character?

Such a question can be asked only because of the
one-sidedness of our "classical" musical culture, the mu-
seum and connoisseur atmosphere that surrounds it, the
fact that the living composer is given no reasonable function that he can play in American life. Composed music
tends to be over cerebral; the composer, not given any
living purpose that his music can serve, invents purely
intellectual forms and systems. His music tends to be
over personalized, the composer not feeling himself part
of the mainstream of humanity, and expressing his resentment against a society which makes no place for him.
Or else it tends to imitate and refine upon the past.

As against this one-sidedness, jazz reasserts the truth

that the creation of art is a social function; that music should be made for people to use. Even if this use is narrowed down to that of dance and song, the fact that the music is meant so to be used gives it vitality and meaning to its listeners.

Jazz reasserts the fact that music is something people do, as well as listen to; that art is not to be limited to a specialized profession, but should be in the possession of everybody. It restores the "amateur" creation that must be part of every culture if it is to be a healthy one. It restores creative music and musical creation to the people. It proclaims that music is one of the means through which people live, as well as make a living. It reveals how deep are the desire and the love for music among people, and how great are their creative resources. It proves, not that elaborate technique and knowledge are unimportant, for they are, but that they are not essential; that if people can get or make any musical instruments, they will learn how to handle them, and if they have no instruments, they will use their voices; that music is a language of human communication, and that people, if given any opportunity, will always make of it something that becomes great art, for it contains living emotion, the felt presence of a human being.

Although jazz is loved and performed by people of every national background, in America the groundbreaker, leader and innovator in every step forward of jazz has been the Negro. The reason is not that the Negro is physically gifted in rhythm above other people, as some proclaim. It lies rather in the basic truth that beauty is a product of labor. In other words, people learn most about art by doing it. The Negro people in their enforced poverty, have had to make their own entertainment, instead of buying it, and getting it predigested and spoon-fed. Other Americans have paid the price for the luxury of a bought entertainment and art, that of being dulled in their creative powers. And dulled in their creative powers, they have been dulled in their ability to enjoy and understand music. The Negro people have also paid a price for having been forced upon their own resources. They have been forced into the limitations of a folk art, limitations which are very real and against which they have rightly rebelled. But at least, within these limitations, they have created a music of phenomenal strength and beauty.

Furthermore, the Negro people, who have been the most oppressed and exploited among us, have had a powerful and terrible story to tell, the telling of which in more explicit languages has been denied to them by repression and censorship. Jazz is a music of protest against discrimination and Jim Crow. It expresses anger at lynchings and at direct or indirect slavery, resentment of poverty. It expresses the hope and struggle for freedom, the vitality which enables a people to wrest joy out of misery and to assert the triumph of human beings over the obstacles which would grind them down. Always the Negro musician has had this story to tell. In the spirituals it was the love of freedom and the struggle against slavery. In the young musician's music of bebop, it is not hard to find the bitter experiences of the American Negro soldier in the past war, Jim-Crowed and treated as a second-class citizen, while he was told that the war was one for democracy, the rights of all people to the "four freedoms."

Precisely because the Negro people speak so powerfully in jazz, it has become loved and admired by all peoples. It discloses the qualities, universal to all people, of anger at oppression and triumph over misery. It sends shoots in all directions, and strikes roots in the strangest soil. It is always one step ahead of its scholars, tabulators and critics. Just as they think they have it nailed down and classified, it comes forth with a new and challenging growth. It is as powerful and unpredictable as the human being himself. It is a gift of the Negro people to America, one that should be a prized cultural treasure.

Its importance to American musical life cannot be overestimated. It has provided America with a musical language rich in human images, emotions embodied in sound; a language that composers can draw upon as fruitfully as the great composers of the past drew upon the folk and popular music of their time. It points the way to a time when the artificial distinction between "classical" and "popular" will disappear; when music will take on different and varied forms, forms of song and dance and forms of powerful drama or psychological complexity. But all forms will be equally accessible to people, and the only questions to be asked will be, is it good music or bad? Is it honest music or dishonest? Does it give us pleasure to know it? Does it help us to know better our fellow human beings and the world which we share with them?

CHAPTER TWO

THE SOUND OF JAZZ

he primary quality which causes jazz to sound different from classical music, or sweet, tin-pan-alley music, is its use of the instrument. The jazz approach to the instrument is the opposite to the one with which we are generally familiar. According to the common conception, the music suggests the instrumentation. In jazz, the instrument creates the outlines of the music.

31

It is not hard to discover how we get our one-sided conception of the relation between music and the instrument. The tendency of nineteenth century classical music was to erase from the listener's mind all consciousness of the medium of expression, and instead to arouse in the mind a sense of pictorial color or shifting psychological mood. Whether the music was intended to be thundering or ethereal, the instrumentation had to be of a pervading sweet sensuousness enabling the composer to soothe or captivate the listener. Out of the demands of this music a new kind of performer arose, a virtuoso who had to spend finger-breaking years of training simply to be able to handle the piano so that all trace of percussiveness should be eliminated, or the violin so that there should never be a scratch or harsh tone, or the orchestra so that its massed tone should rise and swell like disembodied sound. This approach to musical sound, seeking to banish from the listener's ear all consciousness of the instrument, produced its own fine, if one-sided instrumental lore. It arrives at its final absurdity in the practise of tin-pan-alley, Broadway and Hollywood, where the "arranger" orchestrates the music supplied by the "composer," as if orchestration and the actual sound of the music were nothing more than the application of some standard rules that anyone could master from a textbook.

But the instrumentation of a music, its final clothing in sound, is as much a part of a composer's thinking as its melodies. And while the science of orchestration, the relation between instrumental timbre and harmony, is an important part of musical knowledge, the fundamental law of musical creation, whether in composed music or jazz, is that the instrument suggests the music. Throughout the history of music it has always been a new instrument that made a new music possible, and this is the basis of jazz instrumentation.

We can understand the logic of this approach better when we analyze what a musical instrument is. It is an extension of the human hand and voice, a tool which adds new powers to the human mind and new subtleties to human senses. Just as the invention of the hammer and axe opened up to human beings new possibilities of satisfying their wants, so the creation and mastery of musical instruments opened up new possibilities of creating and using the language of organized sound. This relation of the instrument to music was understood by practically all composers up to fairly recent times. It was for his grasp of the possibilities of each instrument that Mozart remains unequalled as an orchestrator, even in these days of grandiose symphony orchestras and seemingly infinite variation of sound.

The jazz treatment of the musical instrument strikes listeners, by contrast, as harsh or strident. Yet this feeling of harshness or roughness is basic to the expressive quality of jazz. When we hear people speak, we are actually listening to what would musically be harsh tones, even in a well modulated voice. Yet we don't get a sensation of harshness. In fact, a person who spoke in an almost musically pitched voice, as some actors do, would annoy us after a few minutes. Sweetness of sound was never, except in some special periods of music, a criterion of artistic quality. Expressiveness and communication is rather the criterion, and expressiveness is a matter of contrasts, of the subtle interplay of opposite timbres and colors. If we call the roughness of jazz sound "primitive," it is only because we are misled by the "old master" mellowness of most concert music heard today.

Much of the Negro music of the past century was crude, which is another thing than primitive; and even this word must be used in a limited sense. It was a music created by untrained voices, and whatever rough instruments could be made, or found at hand; the jug band, washboard for percussion, the banjo, one string violin, harmonica. But the music created was a highly subtle music within its limitations for it had something to say.

The limitations of this music were very real. If we listen to a group of folk-spiritual singers, for example, we find that while the music is very beautiful, the group knows only a few basic melodic and harmonic patterns. The consciousness of these limitations, the desire to experiment with new possibilities, the desire for fuller life and expression has been the basis of all progress in folk music and jazz, although it is not understood by some connoisseurs who, jaded with "too much" civilization, rush back to the arms of the "primitive." The Negro musician has created great forms of music in America and always abandoning one when he had no need for it, and moving on to another, even into symphony and opera. Nor has he paid much attention to those who accused him of thus abandoning "the genius of his race."

With the slowly growing and constantly obstructed improvement of the conditions of Negro life, after the Civil War, new instruments were adopted, and these helped create a new quality of music. These instruments were first those of the military band, many of them Confederate Army instruments now to be found in pawnshops; trumpets, cornets, trombones, clarinets, tubas, bass and snare drums. The banjo, a favorite instrument of plantation, minstrel show and wandering blues singers, was added to the band, slowly replaced in later times by the guitar. The piano, found in the better-off homes, and in saloons and dance halls, came into prominent use, producing a variety of sounds fresh to the ear and true to the basic percussive character of the instrument. Later acquisitions were the string bass, replacing the tuba, and the saxophone.

In sketching, then, a history of jazz through its instrumentation, we can say that the music of slavery was predominantly choral, with a dance music made up of any crude instruments adaptable to musical use. The emancipation after the Civil War, with its comparatively greater freedom of movement, brought the choral work song, and the solo voice of the blues with instrumental accompaniment. The life of the Negro community in the Southern city between the 1890's and 1920's, a restricted, "ghetto" life, but on a higher level of course than slavery, brought a communal music of dance and parade, in which each instrument was handled as a solo voice, but all combined together in brilliant interplay of melodic lines. This last, in general, is called "New Orleans" music, for in New Orleans this city music reached its freest development.

The next step in emancipation, the struggle against the semi-slavery of Southern life and the growing northward migration, brought a new step in jazz instrumentation; the formation and leadership of large bands, so that the band itself became an instrument rich in possibilities for the creative musician. Basic to the formation of this band was the use of the saxophone choir, of alto, tenor and baritone. It is customary, among some jazz critics, to frown upon the formation of these large bands, as an intrusion of "symphonic" music into the "purity" of jazz. Yet these large bands of brass, reed and percussion, in the hands of a Lunceford or Ellington, are magnificent musical combinations, new to our culture, and the full possibilities of which are far from explored. It is important to remember, in discussing the history of jazz, that nothing of value is ever really lost. It is only the one-sidedness of our musical life today, a direct product of commercialism, which uses the "new" to wipe out the "old," and thus impels others to propagandize for the old against the new. A musical instrument is an extension of the voice and mind, as a tool is an extension of the hand and mind. An instrument, like a tool, makes possible deeper and richer creation, so long as one remembers that it has no meaning in and by itself, without the human being behind it.

First of jazz instruments is the human voice, which is of course the major instrument in all music history. There has not been any age or musical culture without its own typical vocal music. It was out of the inflections of the speaking human voice that music as song originated, just as it was out of the movements of the human body that music as rhythm originated.

In the most simple folkish blues we can hear a music that is part speech, part song. One can almost speak these blues, and in fact the singer seems often to be speaking. This may seem to be a crude form of music, and it has its limitations. The scale, or basic pattern of musical notes, employed by these blues, resembles the five-note, or pentatonic scales used by other folk music cultures. Such simpler scales were made necessary by the limited possibilities of the untrained human voice, and in fact were a creation of the voice. People are not born with the ability to control their voices down to the fine pitch demanded by our system of whole or half tones. More elaborate scales were made possible by the invention of musical instruments on which man could establish and manipulate pitch with scientific accuracy. It was only by training, along with such instruments, that the modern singer's voice was made possible; and in operatic coloratura numbers we can still hear a flute (or a trumpet, as in Handel's time) leading the way for the voice to follow.

Yet if the simple scale of the blues, and the song that is semi-speech, are inadequate for a complete musical culture, they have a quality which is worth retaining in a musical culture, the practise of amateur music making. It is important to have a kind of musical performance in which people can take part and even create without professional training. And if blues singing seems to be a technically limited art, it requires an artistry of its own all the more important because it depends upon inner human resources, a capacity for the dramatization and projection of a human personality. The art of a Leroy Carr or Huddle Leadbetter (Leadbelly) is not easy to duplicate; and if neither can do what a trained opera singer does, the opera singer cannot duplicate what they do.

When we come to the "classic" style of blues singing, the art of a Ma Rainey, Bessie Smith, Clara Smith, Bertha Hill, we are entirely out of the amateur class of music making. Bessie Smith sings completely on pitch, when she wants to. The off-pitch "blue note," a product of the blues scale, is used with the most controlled and deliberate artistry. Its role is to intensify the bond between poetry and music, so that it gives to certain words an especially poignant and "speaking" quality. Throughout her performance there are other such subtle, planned or felt out, deviations from pitch, and slides or glissandos, which similarly add speaking inflections to the voice.

In blues singing the art is to put over the words as well as the melody, but here we are in a type of art which has never left the history of music. In the great motet and madrigal art of medieval times, Renaissance Italy and Elizabethan England, the beats or accents were not guided by the bar lines, as in modern music, but by the accents of the poetry, so that the most fascinating cross rhythms resulted. The operas of Monteverdi, the religious works of Schuetz and Bach used a free melodic "recitative" line in which the accents of speech guided the rendering of the music. Singers of folk music who really know the medium, such as Yvette Guilbert, Victor Chenkin and Elsie Houston, use speech sounds and speech inflections with the most delightful artistry. And even in performing Schubert's songs or Verdi's arias, the singer who does not understand that the rhythms, inflections and accents of speech are an organic part of the music will give a mechanical and wrong performance.

With the rise of the popular song in the idiom of jazz, the voice took on a new role. In the singing of Louis Armstrong and "Fats" Waller a frequent deliberate harshness serves as a sardonic commentary on the idiocy of the words and the sugariness of the tune. Louis' "scat" singing, of nonsense syllables, make this point clear, for since the words are really meaningless, why use them? At the other extreme, singers like Ella Fitzgerald and Billie Holiday make an art of consciously putting over the words, as well as the tune. The songs however, unlike the more honest and meaningful material that Bessie Smith used, being generally false, shallow concoctions in word and music, are hampering to the singers. Consequently they must create a personal singing style, without much relation to the song. In Billie's case, this style is made up of an entrancing tone color, a subtle slurring of pitch, a suspenseful delayed attack and a partial transformation of the melodic line into a blues line. Finally, with Sarah Vaughan, we have a singing style which is a product of the modern chromatic jazz, with its constant change of key and use of half tones and strange intervals. Such singing must be completely on pitch, except for lightly and deliberately slurred notes, for otherwise the effect of the half tones and key changes is lost; and it requires the finest ear training.

Basic, then, to the art of the voice in jazz, is the use of contrasts, the interplay of opposites; song and speech, on-pitch notes and blue-notes, on-pitch notes and movements to surprising intervals and keys. This double or contrasting character of timbre and vocal handling is likewise basic to the entire jazz use of the instrument.

It is probably the drum and percussion battery that, more than any other single jazz instrument, has inspired

the African theories of jazz. But intricate drum and percussion patterns are to be found in all tribal music, in
India, the South Seas, Central Asia and the Americas.
And while the African use of drums is magnificent in its
own right, there is a basic difference between it and the
jazz drum. Much of African drumming was a substitute
for speech, or vocal communication. The rise of more
elaborate melodic instruments, and a more elaborate body
of melody, as in jazz, made such use of the drums and
rhythm unnecessary. Furthermore, even when used as an
accompaniment to dance or chant, African drumming,
for all its intricacy of two or three rhythms at once, has
a single-minded, compelling beat, aimed at fusing all
listeners into one mind and one movement. Jazz drumming is much more modern, "human" in the sense of
never letting us forget that this is a new age in which
the group is made up of more individual, thinking minds.
It is much more elastic in its rhythm. Even when a second
and third rhythmic pattern is laid down against the basic
4/4 beat, the opposing rhythms are never free from one
another, as in African "polyrhythmic" drumming, but
combine in each phrase, like a "going away" and "return
home." Characteristic of jazz drumming, and not found
in African, is the surprise, the kidding, the serious-comic
spirit which pervades all jazz music and creates some of
its most powerful emotional effects; the break, the sudden silence, the suspension of rhythm and return to the
beat. Military marches, as played by the army, are much

closer to the spirit of African drums than jazz is, and if we compare a military march to a New Orleans jazz march like "High Society," we can immediately see the contrast between the hypnotic rhythm of the former, mechanistic in the light of our modern appreciation of the individual human being, and the elastic, human and joyous character of the latter. It is also worth pointing out that African music and culture itself is undergoing a change and development.

In the 'twenties, many composers like Stravinsky in his "Sacre," Milhaud in his "L'Orestie D'Eschyle" music, Ravel in parts of his Concerto for Left Hand, Copland in his Jazz Concerto, employed a polyrhythm close to African music, sometimes under the mistaken idea that they were reproducing jazz. Such music, although it has many other beauties, has a mechanistic, inhuman quality in the light of our present day feelings and needs, a quality neither African nor wholly modern, and never found in jazz. About the only approach to this music in jazz is in some virtuoso drum solos by players with no real feeling for the jazz phrase. Even in the work of Max Roach, the brilliant bebop drummer, who works up the most intricate pattern of cross and interplaying rhythms, there is always the human elasticity, the interplay with and against the basic beat, which is fundamental to jazz, although the suspensions of beat are stretched to fantastic intervals.

The jazz drum, finally, is a social instrument. It has its own role and is, at the same time, part of a group, interplaying with and supporting the other instruments, subtly adjusting its timbres to back and fill out the solos, marking the end of one and introducing another, accenting a climax. Such a use of the drums has some vague precedents in composed music, as in the works of Berlioz and Rimsky-Korsakov, but far below the finesse, the joyous interplay of two musical minds, reached in jazz. "Baby" Dodds, Zutty Singleton, Sidney Catlett, Dave Tough, Joe Jones, George Wettling, Cozy Cole and Max Roach are some of the masters, each in his own style, of this kind of social drumming.

The other percussive instruments, such as banjo, guitar, piano and string bass likewise have both an individual and social role to play. One of the most extraordinary and beautiful achievements of jazz sound is the combined rhythm section, or harmonized percussion; a beat that is at the same time a chord, and a rich-timbred sound. The strumming banjo or guitar is, of course, an old hand at this kind of tuned rhythm, and has parallels to folk instruments like the dulcimer and balalaika, and to the harp in composed music. An invention of jazz, however, was the addition of the plucked string bass, adding to the richness of percussive sound and at the same time providing a harmony. Its tones vary, from the slapping of a "Pops" Foster to the sweeter string tone of an Israel Crosby and John Kirby.

Each of these rhythm instruments has developed a solo role. The banjo, in the hands of a Johnny St. Cyr, has its fine dance-like patterns. The guitar, as Bernard Addison and Teddy Bunn play it, shows its singing blues background, with one-string solos supported by chords. Bass players, like Jimmy Blanton and "Slam" Stewart, returned to the bow, producing a saxophone-inspired kind of melodic solo. But the most splendid and new percussive achievement of jazz was its collective rhythm section, powerful in its beat yet constantly varying in timbre, and adding a rich harmonic support to the solo lines. Through it jazz has restored rhythm as a powerful, independent musical voice in a performance, without the dehumanization that appears in some contemporary composed experiments with rhythm.

The trumpet became the leading instrument about which New Orleans parade music developed, its brilliant timbre and carrying power, its explosive, percussive impact combined with sweet singing tones, making it especially fit for a "lead" role. It took on as well the role of "singing" the blues, and developed a great variety of timbres, combining the open horn with muted, growl and half-valve, cloudy tones. Such "dirty" tones are often ascribed to an attempt to imitate the human voice. Too much can be made of this theory, however, for just as some trumpet timbres are ascribed to a voice influence, some vocal practises, like Armstrong's singing, are ascribed to a "trumpet" technique.

There have been many deliberate attempts to imitate the human voice with the trumpet, as with the clarinet and trombone. But the relation between voice and instrument takes place on a higher level than that of mere imitation. Rather, the trumpet becomes an extension of the human voice, and translates the accents of speech, the staccato consonants and long drawn vowels, into trumpet timbre. These timbres are expansions of possibilities within the trumpet itself, and so jazz, rather than limiting the instrument to vocal imitation, has enormously expanded the technical and expressive possibilities of the instrument.

The purpose of the "dirty" tones, furthermore, is not solely comic, although it may often be so, but the wholly musical one of providing the contrast that makes for expressiveness. They are not meant to be heard alone. Actually a "dirty" tone can get to sound as cloyingly sweet as the open horn, and more so. Surprise and contrast, either with itself or with other instruments, are the secret of the moving music created by the jazz trumpet; the New Orleans parades, demanding a percussive impact together with a clear melodic line, and the blues, calling for the utmost in expressive nuances, made a major musical instrument of the trumpet, raising it to a level not found in the previous history of music; although it is interesting to notice that in some almost forgotten eras of music, the trumpet was given a major role. The Gabrielis in Renaissance Venice used it lavishly

in their public festival music; and again, with the rise of
opera, the trumpet took on a major instrumental role.
"In the Venetian opera symphony (overture) in the
latter half of the seventeenth century, trumpeters ruled
the orchestral roost, flourishing forth in brilliant solos
and duets against the more thickly massed, more slowly
paced orchestral body. Sacred music as well as secular
felt the virtuoso's presence, and in the church sonatas and
symphonies, no less than in the operatic overtures, trumpet solos and duets were by no means uncommon." [1]
This also, incidentally, happened to be an age in which
improvisation was much more accepted a part of a musical performance than in composed music today. But it
is safe to say that no music of the past produced the
variety of trumpet tones found in jazz.

The history of New Orleans jazz revolves mainly
about its trumpet players such as Buddy Bolden, Fred
Keppard, Joe "King" Oliver, Bunk Johnson. Many fine
trumpet players who rose to prominence in later days,
like Louis Armstrong, Tommy Ladnier, Mutt Carey,
Lee Collins and Joe Smith, are a product of New Orleans
tradition. It is upon the New Orleans tradition that the
"Chicago" and "Dixieland" trumpet players draw, such
as Max Kaminsky, Yank Lawson, "Wild" Bill Davison,
Billy Butterfield, "Muggsy" Spanier. Two who helped
bring "modern" jazz into being, each in his own way,

[1] Abraham Veinus, *The Concerto,* Garden City, N. Y., Doubleday Doran, 1944, p. 9.

were "Bix" Beiderbecke and Frank Newton. Even in the days of the large band, when the saxophone threatened to take the leadership of jazz, much of the changing history of the Ellington band can be told in terms of its trumpet players: "Bubber" Miley, Arthur Whetsel, "Cootie" Williams, Rex Stewart. The Basie band produced Buck Clayton, Shad Collins, Harry Edison. Today, the honors for ushering in bebop are divided between Charlie Parker's alto sax and "Dizzy" Gillespie's trumpet.

New Orleans trombone, like the trumpet, had a social role to play. It unfolded a bass harmonic and melodic voice under the trumpet's lead, and added a rhythmic punch of its own. In this role it developed its own natural, contrasting timbres; long, sustained tones and slides, or glissandos, that gave it stunning percussive power. It likewise sang the blues often with a rough, expressive burr to its tone, contrasting to a sweet vibrato. And, at the same time, it embodied the boisterous, joyous and comic spirit of the parade band, hitting the lowest note on its register as the upper instruments were rising, sliding into a powerful blasting note as if to urge the other instruments to answer. "Tailgate" trombone is the name given to the sustained and percussive, rough and sweet parade role of the instrument. Some of its masters are Edward "Kid" Ory, Preston Jackson, Charlie Green, George Brunis, Jim Robinson. In later days the trombone took on a more predominantly solo role, but still used its vibrato, its rough and sweet contrasts, its subtle play with pitch, to poignantly mold and color a blues line. Jack Teagarden, Benny Morton, "Tricky" Sam Nanton and Lawrence Brown of Ellington's band, Miff Mole, Jimmy Harrisson, Sandy Williams, J. C. Higginbotham, Dicky Wells, J. J. Johnson and Vic Dickenson are some of those who kept the tradition of the instrument as a major jazz voice.

The clarinet was the virtuoso of New Orleans music, like the coloratura soprano in Italian opera. Unlike the trumpet and trombone, which took on new and important roles in later jazz, the clarinet has tended in the modern large band to become an accessory to the saxophone. It was mainly in Ellington's music that, inspired by the gifts of Barney Bigard, the clarinet was assigned a large-band musical role distinctively its own.

Like the other instruments in New Orleans music, the clarinet developed a social role. Inspired perhaps by the piccolo parts of the military marches, it added a dancing upper voice and brilliant decorative figures to the trumpet's lead. It was, at the same time, a fine singing blues instrument, making full use of its great range, its contrasts of tone between low and high register, its glissandos, its sweet and rough timbres. Particularly beautiful, in New Orleans rag and stomp performances, are its long, slow melodic phrases, contrasting in accent and tempo to the fast trumpet lead. Johnny Dodds and Sidney Bechet are particular masters of this most moving

kind of blues and off-beat playing, and New Orleans life and tradition produced many other clarinet masters: Alphonse Picou, "Big-Eye" Louis Nelson, Albert Nicholas, Omer Simeon, Jimmy Noone, Edmund Hall, Larry Shields, Leon Rappolo, George Lewis. Barney Bigard is a New Orleans product. In fact, New Orleans jazz has given the clarinet its richest body of music since Mozart made such wonderful use of the instrument in his clarinet concerto, chamber works and divertimentos. In more recent jazz, the main innovators on the clarinet were Frank Teschemacher and "Pee Wee" Russell, who used a reedy tone, harsh and without vibrato, and Benny Goodman, who brought to jazz a concert-hall beauty of tone and fluidity of technique.

The saxophone figured little in New Orleans music. Sidney Bechet adopted the soprano sax, and achieved a feat with it almost comparable to that of Louis Armstrong with the trumpet, making the one instrument self-supporting by taking on a two-voiced role. Where Louis combined a "lead" melody with accompanying arpeggios or broken chords, Bechet combined the New Orleans clarinet decoration with the staccato trumpet-like lead possible on the heavier voiced sax.

It was with the rise of the large band, however, that the saxophone became a central instrument of jazz. The alto, tenor and baritone saxes filled the same role as the quartet of strings in the rise of the symphony orchestra; a body of instruments, homogeneous in tone, which could form the harmonized basis for the musical structure. And, with the growing importance of the saxophone in jazz, the instrument developed a solo style as well.

To some purists, the saxophone has become a symbol for commercialism; and it is true that the sax, alone and in combination, can afflict the ear with the most cloyingly sweet, ersatz music. But in modern jazz, as in the past, and indeed as in the history of all music, the quality of what is produced depends upon the human being who produces it. The jazz performer with honesty and taste has been able to give any instrument musical distinction, even a slide whistle. The saxophone, like the trumpet, trombone and clarinet, has become a major musical instrument. Coleman Hawkins gave the tenor sax a completely unsentimental solidity and beauty of tone, shading it with the utmost refinement and alternating sustained melodic phrases with powerful staccato and percussive passages. Ben Webster, Leon "Chu" Berry and Don Byas created a saxophone style fit for anyone to hear, and Lester Young, giving the instrument a cloudier and huskier tone, has created about as moving a music as anybody in the past ten years. In his playing, even more than Hawkins', there is a fine contrast of timbres, a constant interplay of roughness and sweetness.

The alto sax, in the wrong hands, can be even more sickly and sentimental than the tenor. Benny Carter, Willie Smith and Tab Smith however, among others, have given it a strong, clean-cut tone, fit to carry a musical thought; Johnny Hodges has made it speak with all the inflections of a human voice; and Charlie Parker has made it a fine virtuoso instrument. The rise of saxophone jazz, of course, was accompanied by the increasing entrance of the popular song idiom into jazz; a wholly different kind of music from the blues, which brought the jazz musician a host of new problems to solve. In coping with these problems a new kind of music was brought into being, of mixed qualities. The problem of an idiom in present-day jazz is still far from settled. But it is undeniable that, in the development of the saxophone, the world of music has gained another major instrument, the full possibilities of which only jazz has so far explored.

The jazz piano, like the piano of classical or composed music, has created a music wholly its own, although it also enters into the most interesting combinations with other instruments. In the case of the piano, so great has its development been in the history of music, that one cannot say jazz has broken new instrumental ground. Yet it is interesting to notice that jazz in its own independent growth created many styles which parallel, in their approach to instrumental sound, the most varied achievements of learned composers.

In general there are three approaches to piano tone found in jazz, although these divisions are not exact and overlap in the work of actual performers. One of them is the blues and stomp piano, also known as "barrelhouse" and "boogie-woogie." It creates a richly melodic as well as rhythmic music in both the left hand and the right, building magnificent sonorities, intensified by the frequent use of clashing dissonances. It makes a fine use of what classical composers would call "registration," the contrasts in tone color at various keyboard levels. It makes a rich use of guitar figures, such as trills and tremolos for sustained tones and rapid broken chords. There are parallels between this piano and Bach's use of the keyboard in the more boisterous dance movements of his suites, and also interesting parallels to the harpsichord music of Domenico Scarlatti. Scarlatti made a prolific use of Spanish lute figures in his harpsichord style, and it is an enlightening lesson in music history to compare a work like Meade Lux Lewis' "Honky Tonk Train" to Scarlatti's "Les Adieux," the one adapting guitar figures and the other lute figures to the keyboard instrument. There are also obvious parallels between blues and stomp piano, and the percussive use of the instrument by contemporary composers such as Prokofiev and Bartok. Among the masters of this kind of jazz piano are "Pinetop" Smith, Meade Lux Lewis, Jimmy Yancey, Pete Johnson, Albert Ammons, Montana Taylor, and lesser known figures like "Blind" Leroy Garnett and Henry Brown.

A second approach to the piano uses the left hand sparingly, while the right hand embarks upon brilliant melodic and decorative figures. This is also a percussive piano, although the emphasis is less on big sonorities than on sharp and clear note patterns. Ragtime piano, as played by "Jelly-Roll" Morton, is a fine example of this style, and in his work, the left hand takes on a more economical, if musically inventive, role. Out of it have developed many groundbreaking variations. Earl Hines

spins out dazzling rhythmic patterns, attaining a powerful intensity by suspending the basic beat almost to the
breaking point. "Fats" Waller gives the ragtime piano
an almost barrelhouse boisterousness. James P. Johnson
spins imaginative and witty melodic inventions. Teddy
Wilson develops a style of delicate traceries and decorative figures, and carries the melody into strange harmonic channels. Count Basie, at the other extreme, but
likewise using predominantly the right hand, creates a
style of the utmost economy, so that the melody is suggested by widely separated notes and chords.

A third style uses sustained notes and chords, in
somewhat similar fashion to the "romantic" music of
the nineteenth century. Examples of this style are found
in the work of Duke Ellington, Art Tatum, Billy Kyle
and Errol Garner. It is a comparatively recent development, one made possible by the rise of large bands and
the availability of better pianos. Up to now it has far
from explored its full jazz possibilities.

Jazz then, a product of the Negro and the most
exploited people of America, a sign of their imagination,
and inventiveness, their struggle to express themselves
as human beings in life as well as music, has created a
"new sound." Yet part of the fascination of jazz is that
it is also an "old sound." It not only reveals to us the
immense creative resources that lie deep in the common
people. It also teaches us how to listen to music.

For the fact is that a great many classical concert

goers, and musicians as well, do not really know how to listen to music. The music they hear is only a fraction of the great world of created music, and even that is often misinterpreted. The art of music, throughout its history, is one of rich improvisation, joy in exploring the possibilities of the instrument, social and communal music making, the song and dance. It is well known that many listeners, who are brought up in the average concert repertory, find contemporary music harsh and baffling, and are also somewhat baffled by the music of the eighteenth, seventeenth and previous centuries, although more respectful toward it.

Listening to jazz, the song-speech of the blues, the many-voiced structure built out of the blues by jazz improvisors, the expressive harshness and sweetness of the instrumentation, and the contrasts and combinations of timbre, listening to its powerful yet elastic rhythmic beat, making us all feel part of the same family and yet intensifying in us our individual sense of the pain and joy of life, we develop new musical ears. We enjoy the song-speech of the Italian, French and English madrigalists; the instrumental exploration of the Bach and Vivaldi concertos, in which the solo passages are so much like jazz "hot solos"; the love of the instrument in its own natural color found in the concertos and chamber music of Mozart and Haydn. We feel a beat, human, powerful, yet elastic, not too distant from jazz, in much old music; Bach, in his use of dance patterns for some of his most moving arias; Haydn, in the folkish quality of so many of his symphonic movements.

And our ears become opened as well to modern music, for jazz is also one of the great bodies of modern music. Through jazz we can appreciate better the percussive sonorities of the Prokofiev Seventh Piano Sonata, or his happy use of the most unviolinistic, as well as violinistic tones, in his First Violin Concerto; the rich percussive piano, the use of folkish, violin glissandos, the intricate rhythmic patterns, of the Bartok sonatas and concertos; the song-speech of the Ives songs, and the intricate beat of his barn-dance sonata and symphonic movements; the "parade" spirit of the last movement of the Shostakovich Sixth Symphony, so much like a New Orleans march; the experiment with new scales of the Debussy works, and their fine exploration of new instrumental color combinations; the values of Vaughan Williams' use of English folk song in his symphonic works.

Nor is this re-education in music limited to the periods before and after the nineteenth century, the "concert hall" era. We begin to listen to this music as well with new ears. We find in Beethoven's piano more than a little "barrelhouse," as in the last movements of his "Pastoral" Sonata Op. 28, and his "Appassionata," Op. 57; and we appreciate better the revolution in our understanding of Beethoven brought by a scholar like Arthur Schnabel. We find in Schubert a wealth of song and dance music. We find in Chopin not only the dreamy "salon" composer, but the Polish national composer, feeling a folk beat not only in his mazurkas and polonaises but in his nocturnes and studies. We see in Lizst not the exhibitionist some pianists make of him, but the artist testing the full range and powers of an instrument. We appreciate better, instead of decrying as "amateur," the bare, economical instrumentation of Mussorgsky, the powerful "tuned percussion" of the Clock Scene in "Boris Godunov." We see how great a contribution was made to music by Verdi and Chaikovsky, in restoring to music the strong, athletic line of human song.

Jazz has given us a liberal education.

RECORD ILLUSTRATIONS—CHAPTER TWO

BESSIE SMITH
One and Two Blues (Columbia 36281)
With Joe Smith, trumpet; Fletcher Henderson, piano; Buster Bailey, clarinet

BESSIE SMITH
Baby Doll, Lost Your Head Blues (Columbia 35674)
With Joe Smith, trumpet; Fletcher Henderson, piano

BILLIE HOLIDAY
Summertime, Billie's Blues (Columbia 37496)
With Bunny Berigan, trumpet; Artie Shaw, clarinet; Cozy Cole, drums; Joe Bushkin, piano; Dick McDonough, guitar; Pete Peterson, bass

BILLIE HOLIDAY
I Can't Get Started, When a Woman Loves a Man (Columbia 37494)
With Buck Clayton, trumpet; Dickie Wells, trombone; Lester Young, tenor sax; Margaret Johnson and Teddy Wilson, piano; Freddie Green, guitar; Walter Page, bass; Jo Jones, drums

SISTER ROSETTA THARPE AND MARIE KNIGHT
Precious Memories, Beams of Heaven (Decca 48070)
With Sam Price trio

KID RENA'S DELTA JAZZ BAND
Lowdown Blues, Gettysburg March (Circle 1035)
Henry Rena, trumpet; Louis Nelson and Alphonse Picou, clarinet; Jim Robinson, trombone; Willie Santiago, guitar; Albert Gleny, bass; Joe Rena, drums

JOHNNY DODDS
Joe Turner Blues (Brunswick 80075)
Johnny Dodds, clarinet; George Mitchell and Reuben Reeves, trumpet; Gerald Reeves, trombone; Charlie Alexander, piano; Johnny St. Cyr, banjo; "Baby" Dodds, drums

LOUIS ARMSTRONG AND ORCHESTRA

Skid-Dat-De-Dat, Muskat Ramble (Columbia 36153)
Twelfth Street Rag, Knocking a Jug (Columbia 35663)
Savoy Blues, Put 'em Down Blues (Columbia 37537)

Louis Armstrong, trumpet; Johnny Dodds, clarinet; Edward Ory, trombone; Lillian Armstrong, piano; Johnny St. Cyr, banjo— Lonnie Johnson added on "Savoy Blues," on "Knocking a Jug"— Louis Armstrong, trumpet; Jack Teagarden, trombone; "Happy" Cauldwell, tenor sax; Joe Sullivan, piano; Eddie Lang, guitar; Kaiser Marshall, drums

DUKE ELLINGTON AND ORCHESTRA

Black and Tan Fantasy, The Mooche (Brunswick 80002)
Bragging in Brass (Columbia 36276)
Cotton Tail, Don't Get Around Much Any More (Victor 26610)

Duke Ellington, piano; Fred Guy, guitar; Sonny Greer, drums; on all. Wellman Braud, tuba and bass; Bubber Miley, trumpet; featured on "Black and Tan"; Johnny Hodges, alto sax, on "The Mooche"; Rex Stewart trumpet, on "Bragging in Brass"; Ben Webster, tenor sax and Jimmy Blanton, bass, on "Cotton Tail"

McKENZIE AND CONDON'S CHICAGOANS

China Boy (Columbia 35951)

Frank Teschemacher, clarinet; Jimmie McPartland, trumpet; Bud Freeman, tenor sax; Joe Sullivan, piano; Eddie Condon, guitar; Jim Lannigan, bass; Gene Krupa, drums

SIDNEY BECHET'S BLUE NOTE JAZZ MEN

High Society, Jackass Blues (Blue Note 50)

Sidney Bechet, clarinet; Max Kaminsky, trumpet; George Lugg, trombone; Art Hodes, piano; George "Pops" Foster, bass; Fred Moore, drums

FLETCHER HENDERSON AND ORCHESTRA

Stampede (Columbia 35669)

Featuring Joe Smith, Rex Stewart trumpets

A JAM SESSION AT VICTOR

Honeysuckle Rose, Blues (Victor 25559)

Thomas "Fats" Waller, piano; Bunny Berigan, trumpet; Dick Mc-Donough, guitar; Tommy Dorsey, trombone; George Wettling, drums

GEORGE BRUNIES AND HIS JAZZ BAND
Royal Garden Blues, Tin Roof Blues (Commodore 556)

George Brunies, trombone; "Wild" Bill Davison, trumpet; Pee Wee Russell, clarinet; Eddie Condon, guitar; Gene Schroeder, piano; Bob Casey, bass; George Wettling, drums

PEE WEE RUSSELL'S RHYTHMAKERS
Dinah, (HRS 1000)

Pee Wee Russell, clarinet; Max Kaminsky, trumpet; Dicky Wells, trombone; James P. Johnson, piano; Al Gold, tenor sax; Freddie Green, guitar; Zutty Singleton, drums; Wellman Braud, bass

MEZZROW—BECHET QUINTET
Breathless Blues, Evil Gal Blues (King Jazz 147)

Sidney Bechet, Milton "Mezz" Mezzrow, clarinet; Wesley "Sox" Wilson, piano; Wellman Braud, bass; Warren "Baby" Dodds, drums; Coot Grant, vocal, on "Evil Gal"

BECHET-SPANIER BIG FOUR
China Boy, Four or Five Times (HRS 2001)

Sidney Bechet, soprano sax; Francis "Muggsy" Spanier, trumpet; Carmen Mastren, guitar; Wellman Braud, bass

BENNY GOODMAN AND HIS SEXTET
Air Mail Special (Columbia 36720)

Benny Goodman, clarinet; Charlie Christian, guitar; Charles "Cootie" Williams, trumpet; Johnny Guarnieri, piano; George Auld, tenor sax; Arthur Bernstein, bass; Dave Tough, drums

KANSAS CITY SEVEN
Lester Leaps Again, After Theatre Jump (Keynote 1302)

Count Basie, piano; Lester Young, tenor sax; Freddie Green, guitar; Jo Jones, drums; Rodney Richardson, bass; Buck Clayton, trumpet; Dick Wells, trombone

COZY COLE'S ALL STARS
Father Cooperates, Thru For the Night (Keynote 1301)

Earl Hines, piano; Coleman Hawkins, tenor sax; Trummy Young, trombone; Joe Thomas, trumpet; Billy Taylor, bass; Teddy Walters, guitar

RED NORVO AND HIS SELECTED SEXTET
Congo Blues, Get Happy (Comet T-7)

John "Dizzy" Gillespie, trumpet; Charlie Parker, alto sax; Teddy Wilson, piano; "Flip" Phillips, tenor sax; "Red" Norvo, vibraphone; "Slam" Stewart, bass; J. C. Heard, drums

JIM YANCEY
Yancey Stomp, State Street Special (Victor 26589)

MEADE LUX LEWIS
Honky Tonk Train (Decca 18110)

CHARLIE PARKER'S RI-BOP BOYS
Ko Ko (Savoy 597)

Charlie Parker, alto sax; John Gillespie, trumpet and piano; Miles Davis, trumpet; Curly Russell, bass; Max Roach, drums

DEXTER GORDON AND WARDELL GRAY
The Chase (Dial 1017)

Dexter Gordon and Wardell Gray, tenor sax; Red Callender, bass; Chuck Thompson, drums; Jimmy Bunn, piano

This is a list of what are in this writer's opinion all first-class jazz records, which also illustrate the great variety of sound produced by jazz. They are not offered as a selection of the "best" records. For one reason, these are all picked because they are available for purchase, and some of the most beautiful jazz recordings are unfortunately out of print. For another reason, any attempt to choose the "all-time best," or the best trumpet players, piano players, or kazoo players, is a contradiction from the start. A piece of music cannot be graded and assigned a percentage, like a schoolboy's examination paper. There are definite standards of competence by which we can judge jazz performances, and we can also select the music which is alive, fresh and creative, which "jumps," from that which is mechanical or dead. Once these standards are met, and a great number of jazz records meet them, further choice is anybody's pleasure. We seek from works of art what we need from them, and one person's wants are different from another's.

All of the standard jazz instruments are represented, in many different styles and combinations. I thought at first of arranging them according to "voice," "trumpet," "rhythm" and so on, but such a division runs contrary to the character of jazz. Jazz is a social music, and a good performance generally finds all departments doing exhilarating work. I have not tried to include all the outstanding performers on each instrument, and hope to do justice to those left out in some of the listings that follow later chapters. It should also be remembered however, that while all honor is due to the outstanding creative jazz personalities, jazz was brought into being by a whole people, and in the blind ups and downs of the entertainment world, it is only the luckiest who wins fame and is found most prolifically on records.

CHAPTER THREE

THE BLUES AND THE FOLK SONG OF JAZZ

azz" says Eddie Condon, "was always a way of playing music, and its manner —freedom of improvisation on a basic chordal structure—could be applied to any standard song." [1] This definition, that jazz is not a music but only a way of playing music, echoes a standard misconception.

Throughout the Condon book, a racy and enjoyable jazz autobiography, we find Eddie's own definition contradicted. References to the great classic compositions of jazz recur through its pages.

" 'Clarinet Marmalade,' somebody said. Bix nodded and hit the keys. . . . 'All right,' Beiderbecke said,

[1] Eddie Condon and Thomas Sugrue, *We Called it Music,* New York, Holt, 1947, p. 270.

'Panama'. . . . We played all the way to Buffalo—Tiger Rag, Jelly-Roll Blues, Hot Lips, China Boy, Wabash Blues, Royal Garden Blues, Wang Wang Blues, Jazz Me Blues. . . ."

These are only a small part of the body of music beloved by jazz performers and jazz listeners. Jazz is not only a way of playing music but a music itself. And it is a music of most luxuriant melody.

The very nature of jazz texture—it has become a byword that jazz is polyphonic, or many-voiced—places it as one of the most melodic kinds of music, for polyphony is the flowering of melody. It is melody repeated, interweaving with other melody, twisting and doubling upon itself, adding to one voice a second and third, each voice with its own independent song.

Why do we call this most melodic of music "unmelodic," and call the most unmelodic of music, the current tin pan alley output, melodic? The reason is brought out excellently in a passage from Hanns Eisler's "Composing For the Films." He describes the Hollywood (and Tin-Pan-Alley) concept of melody as that of a "tune" so put together that "it is almost possible to guess in advance exactly what will follow. . . . Easy intelligibility is guaranteed by harmonic and rhythmic symmetry, and by the paraphrasing of accepted harmonic procedures; tunefulness is assured by the preponderance of small diatonic intervals."

Such an innocuous concoction of sounds, of which

the best that can be said is that they are not unpleasant, should not be termed "melody," which has too important and honorable a place in the world of music. It should not even be called "sweet," for while the term has become a derogatory one to jazz players, for obvious reasons, yet music can be honorably and movingly sweet, as a great deal of very fine jazz is. The euphonious and predictable arrangement of sounds that Eisler speaks of is the kind of music people want who look on music as something not to listen to; at best a part of background atmosphere, like the perfume wafted in the air of a movie palace. It is also the concept of music held by the hucksters running the music business, who replace quality, which is an art, with quantity, that can be bought. Orchestras are the "best" that money can buy, and a popular tune is made into art by arranging it for a mass of sound rivalling that of a Wagnerian opera. Tunes are put together by hiring specialists to pick the "best" melodic phrases, harmonies and orchestral devices out of the "successful" nineteenth century light opera. Or, if desperate, to pick the brains of mountain singers and blues improvisors, or plagiarize last year's hit tune.

If rhythm or beat is a product of the social function of music, melody is its emotional life. And against the commercially concocted, meaningless euphony, the creative jazzman has always thrown up a free, melodic line full of constant surprise and freshly coined, expressive phrases. The factory system of production of mis-called "popular" music has always regarded the achievement of the musician producing an honest music with jealousy and cupidity; jealousy, because the music produced by one artist trying honestly to express his feelings, even if on a single instrument, has more power than all the elaborate works of the factory, decorated like a Christmas tree with borrowings from the entire late history of music; cupidity because, once the thin, small voice of creative jazz has won a following, it can be lifted, imitated, and blown up into a fortune for everyone else concerned. In this borrowing, of course, the quality of the original is quickly lost.

Creative jazz has style. It applies the test of economy to every note and instrumental sound. It doesn't use a dozen notes where three will do; it doesn't use a dozen instruments when one will adequately handle the melodic line; it doesn't use chords where the melodic feeling fails to call for them. Any element, to be included, must have a meaning, something to say, that would be lost if omitted. And it creates so complete a unity between melodic line, rhythmic beat, accent and instrumental sound that we do not hear these elements separately.

Some commentators have made style into the whole of jazz. Without the hot style there is no jazz, but the hot style by itself is meaningless. Throughout the history of music style of performance has been inseparable from melodic language, as any concert artist finds out who tries to perform a Schubert Symphony, a Brahms Hun-

garian Dance, a Chopin Mazurka, from what he sees in
the notes alone. Every musical work has its own language, demanding a subtle pattern of accents, tone color,
even flexibility of pitch. And each performer adds an
ingredient to the music that is a product of his own personality, just as two performers will play the same
Shakespearian role differently, and yet give a true performance.

Jazz style is a derivation from and inseparable part
of jazz melody. The fundamental melody of jazz is the
blues.

A basic blues melody, put in most simple form, may
be written down as follows:

It is a four-bar phrase, and three such four-bar
phrases make up the twelve-bar blues.

The notes as sung are not exactly the same as they
would sound on the piano, but are "blued." In other
words, every interval in the above melody, every step
from note to note, may be slightly augmented or diminished. Instead of hearing intervals such as we might play
on a piano, we hear intervals dangling between a major
second and a minor third, or between a minor third and
a major third, or between a fourth and a diminished

fifth. These deviations from the pitch familiar to concert music are not, of course, the result of an inability to sing or play in tune. They mean that the blues are a non-diatonic music. Diatonic music is the music of our familiar do-re-mi scales, built on a succession of three whole tones followed by a half tone, and creating a definite sense of key, so that we can transpose the same melody from one key to another. Blues melody is basically without sense of key, nor does it have a sense of "major" and "minor" mode, another characteristic of our diatonic scales. This non-diatonic character, expressed in the blueing of notes and the leap to strange intervals, is an important feature of playing "hot."

Another characteristic of blues melody, making it different from diatonic music, is that the sense of the "octave" is either vague or absent. In the above written melody we can find octaves, such as the high C and low C, or the high F and low F. The feeling of the octave, however, is avoided by accenting or blueing one note and not its fellow.

This description of the blues melody is put down with the full knowledge that it differs from those found in many books on jazz. These studies generally describe the blues as a sequence of chords, such as the tonic, subdominant and dominant seventh. Such a definition, however, is like putting the cart before the horse. There are definite patterns of chords which have been evolved to support the blues, but these do not define the blues, and the blues can exist as a melody perfectly recognizable as the blues, without them. Neither are the blues simply a use of the major scale with the "third" and "seventh" slightly blued or flattened. The fact is that both this explanation, and the chord explanation, are attempts to explain one musical system in terms of another; to describe a non-diatonic music in diatonic terms. The blues may be accompanied by diatonic chords. The blues may even be given a most definite key and octave sense, as follows:

This however, is a "sweetened" blues, a type that rises with the use of the piano in blues performance, or with the mixture of diatonic musical themes with the blues. The difference, however, between the non-diatonic blues and diatonic major-minor music, is the difference between "hot" and "sweet." The blues are not the only non-diatonic system of melody in history. Most folk melodic systems are non-diatonic. While different from jazz, the feeling of freshness and strangeness we get from authentic folk music—Spanish flamenco, for instance, as compared to salon tangos—is a result of the non-diatonic character of the music, comparable to the "hot style" in jazz. The blues, like flamenco and other folk idioms, are a first flowering of human speech into song. These idioms have been overladen by many elaborate musical systems, but have never been wholly swallowed up within them. The blues have never disappeared from jazz, and the word "hot" has evolved to refer to the entrance of the blues phrase, simple yet system-defying, unpredictable in its intonation and movement.

The difference between "hot" and "sweet" is not mentioned in order to argue for pure "hot." There is relatively little pure "hot" music in jazz, and if we heard any pure "hot" music over any length of time our feeling of its great beauty would be alloyed by its narrow range of image. With the growth of instrumental jazz the major part of jazz music has been a fascinating interplay of "hot" and "sweet," non-diatonic and diatonic music. New Orleans jazz, generally upheld as the "pure" jazz, is full of such interplay of two melodic languages, of melodies and chords in a definite major or minor mode, and "sweet" sound, followed by a blues phrase. The point to remember, however, is that this is not a chance mixture but a most careful, conscious and musical use of two languages, interplaying with one another. And this practise, incidentally, is the one followed by most contemporary composers using folk scales and melodies.

Another characteristic of the blues melody is that it is made up of two contrasting melodic lines, a "statement" and "answer." The melody printed above as the "blues" starts on a weak beat, and then covers only two bars and a part of a third. As the melody reaches its lowest point, an answering melody rises. This is technically known as antiphonal music. It is impossible to extract one of these parts from the other and still preserve the blues feeling, just as the living organism can be analyzed down to the cell, but once the cell is broken down we do not have a living organism. The statement and answer is the cell-structure of the blues. Out of this character of the blues cell come the infinite improvisational possibilities, which enable the blues to flower into so amazingly rich and inventive a music. New melodic answers rise to the same statement, and different statements bring the same answer.

Still another characteristic of the blues is its lack of a rigid bar limitation. Actually, in referring to the blues as "twelve-bar," or made up of "four-bar" phrases, we are, as in the case of blues harmony, describing one musical language in terms of another. It is a convenient method of description if, at the same time, we recognize its limitations. The blues are actually a much more rhythmically fluid music than the bar-division implies. If we examine even the simple blues melody written above, we can see that the melody flows outside the bar division. To say that it starts on a "weak" or "off" beat implies that there are really two contrasting sets of beats. Similarly the second "four-bar" statement starts on an off-beat in the last bar of the first answer. And this is true not only for the entire twelve bars, but for an entire blues performance, whether vocal or wholly instrumental.

We can call this organic use of the off-beat "syncopation," but it is actually a more subtle pattern of rhythm. Even syncopation implies a rigid and definite off-beat contrasted to a strict on-beat rhythm. The Dixieland two-to-the-bar beat, and the "jump" style, like the European polka, are nearer to familiar syncopation, and anyone familiar with jazz knows how monotonous either one can sound if not flexibly handled. It would be more accurate to say that our familiar bar lines, like our scales, octaves and major-minor keys, are arbitrary, useful but limited convention which we apply to the blues to fit them into our traditional musical thinking. The subtle "dragging" or "pushing" of the beat is another characteristic of the "hot style." Actually, like the blue note, it is a characteristic of blues melody.

The blues are not rhythmically wild or disorganized. They have a regular, recurrent beat, but it is elastic and fluid. It may be stretched or contracted. It is antiphonal, like blues melody, its basic "cell-structure" implying two beats, not one, which play against each other and flow across bar lines to make each blues performance an unbroken unit. An analysis of a jazz performance by bar groups is a fascinating problem. It can be done, but only with many reservations. Johnny Dodds will often change from a sixteen to a twelve-bar pattern. Many of Bessie Smith's performances do likewise; and a record like "One and Two Blues" exhibits a reshuffling of bar groupings that enable her to build up a masterly, dramatic climax. The performances of Earl Hines and Jimmy Yancey on the piano, Lester Young on the tenor sax, provide similar examples of such freedom from bar limitations. Bebop music, which has a strong blues content, plays havoc with bar lines, the solos always starting somewhere in the middle of the bar and on an off beat, ending somewhere in the middle of a bar, placing their accents always where most unexpected.

It is worth digressing to note that this freedom from strict bar limitations is not unkown to other music, but is a reassertion of a basic truth of music, a "humanization" of music such as I have discussed in previous pages in dealing with rhythm. The great recitative, chanson and madrigal art of early musical centuries shows a similar flexibility, and interplay of beats.

Mussorgsky's songs change their rhythmic pattern from bar to bar, so that an attempt to fit them to traditional bar lines forces the time signature to change from one bar to the next. In our own time Charles Ives writes with a similar abhorrence of strict bar lines. His music looks highly complex on paper, but so would a blues performance if written down exactly. In actual performance, by artists who feel the style, the music should sound as uncomplicated as a good blues performance.

The melody I have written down as typical blues will never be heard, note for note, in any actual blues.

Every performance has its own subtleties of beat and accent, of intonation, melodic variation, addition of other melodic phrases. I offer it, however, as close to "basic" blues; it is a most simple arrangement of notes in a four-bar pattern which, when played, will immediately be recognized as the blues. It displays the non-octave and non-diatonic character of the blues. Any blues melodic line will have some phrase paralleling one of the phrases in the melody above.

This blues melody, the basis of innumerable blues performances, has two characteristics which establish it as a powerful addition to the world musical heritage. It is, first, in itself, a melody of the greatest beauty, one of the world's fundamental and haunting folk songs. Secondly, it is capable of infinite variability.

The blues phrases may be inverted, turned upside down, rising instead of falling. "Trouble in Mind" is an extremely beautiful example of a blues starting with such inverted figures. Johnny Dodds' solo in "Wild Man Blues," Louis Armstrong's opening phrases in his "Knocking a Jug" solo, Picou's solo in the Kid Rena "Lowdown Blues," are other fine examples.

The blues line may be simplified down to a range of as few as four or five notes, giving the performance a concentrated, driving intensity. Sometimes the entire performance seems to gravitate about one recurrent, climactic note. King Oliver's classic "Dippermouth" solo is a masterly example. Or, instead of this staccato repetition of a short phrase, an equally powerful effect can be gotten by one note sustained or repeated for two bars, almost to the breaking point, creating, instead of the previous driving intensity, an equally affecting suspense. This is also a kind of inversion, playing the blues "back-wards," starting the phrase instead of ending it with a long, held note. The Miley trumpet solo in Ellington's "Black and Tan Fantasy" is a fine example, and the rec-ords of Louis Armstrong, Johnny Dodds, Sidney Bechet, provide many others.

The boiling down of the blues melody to a phrase of five, four, three and even two notes, is the foundation of one of the most amazing inventions of jazz performance, the "break." The "break" has generally been described in jazz studies as a rhythmic effect. The break, however, is more than rhythmic play. It is blues melody, concen-trated down to a simplicity beyond which melody can-not go and remain melody. It is true that, in the hands of an uninspired performer, the break may degenerate into mere rhythmic trickiness, or follow a standard pat-tern. In the hands of men like Joe Oliver, Louis Arm-strong, Johnny Dodds, Kid Ory, Sidney Bechet, Charlie Parker, however, the break is a sudden sprout of melody capable of the most exuberant joy and deepest sadness. In many ragtime performances it is mainly through the breaks that the blues language enters. The breaks illus-trate, better than any other aspect of jazz, the distinction between true, expressive melody and a euphonious tune.

There is nothing in the break to suggest a tune; no repetition of phrase, no chord, no suggestion of harmonic sweetness. What remains is melody at its most free, creative, surprising and emotionally expressive, concentrated within the single span of a musical bar.

The riff is comparable to the break, in that it is also blues melody simplified down to a single phrase. Its character and function, however, are completely opposite. It is a structural device, its repetitions of the same phrase over and over again providing a foundation against which solo melodic voices can soar freely. Like every other element of jazz, the riff can be vulgarized. In insensitive hands, it becomes a confession of musical poverty. In the hands of sensitive musicians, like Jelly-Roll Morton, King Oliver, Duke Ellington, Count Basie, it becomes the medium for a relaxed, touching, beautifully organized music, sometimes changing through a performance so that two and three riffs interplay.

The break and riff are the two opposites of blues jazz performance. Where the break is meant to be exciting, to concentrate all attention on itself, the riff is unobtrusive, laying a base for the solo or building up suspense. The break tends to be the blues at their hottest, most succinct and economical in its note pattern, most blue in its intonations and offbeat in its accent. The riff tends to be the blues at their nearest to sweet, diatonic music and nearest to the basic beat. Where the break announces the strange and unusual, the riff brings back the familiar quotation. The break is the fresh, bold improvisation of blues jazz; the riff its common coin, its well-loved folk strain.

The non-diatonic character of the blues melodic language permits it to create most rich and exciting musical textures, of two or three melodic lines moving against each other. These are sometimes described in academic terminology as "polytonal," or using two keys at once. The description, while handy, is not really accurate. Blues improvisation cannot use two keys, since it knows no keys. Blues melody, with its use of seconds, thirds, fourths and fifths, and ability to blue all of these intervals, can literally move anywhere on the musical tonal map. What we would call "dissonances" are frequently struck off. These are not real dissonances, however, but familiar blues intervals. It is only in later jazz, particularly that of Ellington and bebop, where there is a deliberate harmonization of melody and setting of key feeling, that we can properly talk of the use of two keys at once, or polytonality. This has produced a fascinating new music.

When we understand the special character of the blues as a musical language, and its importance to jazz, then we can also begin to understand how important to jazz are the non-blue elements, the other musical languages and systems which jazz absorbed in its development.

The blues are a great social and personal music; social in that they are the language creation of an entire people; personal in that they bring to a performance the musical play of the individual thinking and feeling human being, with a constant strangeness and surprise, laughter and sadness. The blues are inseparable from jazz. Without them, jazz would become mechanical, "corn" or "commercial." Jazz, however, has constantly absorbed and made the richest use of new musical materials, systems and languages. It was by such a process that African strains developed into the spirituals; that the blues developed into the profoundly moving and joyous New Orleans music of song, dance and parade; that New Orleans music evolved into the jazz we have today.

This process of growth, by which two different elements combine to produce a new creation, is not unique to jazz. It is true of all human and natural growth; the manner in which new plants come into being, in which new people come into being, in which nations, languages and cultures come into being. It is the process of growth of all folk music. Not only jazz but other folk music cultures have given rise to wild and unscientific theories of "purity" in music. Purity in music, however is as much a myth as purity when applied to the outmoded term of "race." There just isn't any such thing.

A great advance was made in the study of jazz when it was discovered that jazz has many aspects of a folk music. One of the best descriptions of how folk music grows and changes is that given by A. A. Lloyd, in "The Singing Englishman."

"The songs were learned by ear, remember, and as they spread from village to village across the country and down the ages, they were changing all the time. Lapses of memory would leave gaps which needed new verses to fill them in; bits of other songs, words or tunes, would creep in by accident or intention; singer after singer would modify or embellish the song; till by the time it had spread two hundred miles and been sung for two hundred years, so much would be lost and so much would be added that often the original song would be impossible to distinguish among a thousand variants; and sometimes the variants were so different from the original that they were really quite new songs." [1]

This explains why folk songs of the same land may differ from one another, and yet stem from the same roots; why so many variants exist, with no one variant the "real" song any more than another. The process of change and variation is basic to folk music. Our Negro spirituals show the same characteristics. "Go Down, Moses," "Keep Your Hand on that Plow," "Were You There When They Crucified my Lord," spring from the same root, although they have become quite different and beautiful songs. The rise of a wealth of blues songs from a few germ phrases, and the rise of New Orleans

[1] A. A. Lloyd, *The Singing Englishman,* London, Workers' Music Association, p. 13.

instrumental music out of the rags and blues, shows a similar process.

Lloyd also describes the reverse process, equally necessary to an understanding of the growth of folk art; that of absorption and assimilation.

"To the English folk singer the modes were no mere survival from the past, they were his natural idiom; and when he learned a composed song, even a music hall song, he would often alter the tune till it corresponded to one or another of the familiar modes of English folk music." [1]

This point should be carefully studied. It does not mean that everything new was transformed into the old. It means that out of the union of new and old, a new music came into being. If we don't understand this process, we will not understand why, although we can trace a definite line of continuity in folk music, this music shows such constant change and growth. Both of these aspects of folk music, the germination from a few basic sources and the cross-fertilization and enrichment from many sources, are essential to the understanding of folk music, jazz, and in fact any music.

When we understand this folk character of jazz we can begin to understand the opposite truth; that jazz has characteristics wholly different from folk music, as heretofore known. Jazz is a late nineteenth and twentieth century development. In their creation of a city music,

[1] *Ibid.,* p. 18.

the Negro people used a richer variety of instruments, and thus created a music of greater complexity of texture, than that of European folk music cultures. In the twentieth century the place of the Negro people in relation to American life underwent rapid changes. Factors were the impact of the first World War, the entrance of the Negro into industry, the movement North, the rising struggle against lynching and "legal" lynching by prejudiced police and courts, the formation of large Negro communities in Northern cities with a relatively higher standard of living, the demand of the Negro people for education, freedom of movement, the right to hold governmental office and enter all jobs and professions open to anyone else. Finally there was the impact of the second World War, which brought to a head the contradictory treatment of the Negro people in a country which held itself up as a model of democracy.

As changes affected the Negro musician and Negro audience, the music rapidly changed. Compared to other folk cultures, whose development is slow and spans centuries, jazz shows a tremendously rapid tempo of change. The result is that the jazz musician is faced today with problems that almost exactly parallel those of the "learned" composer, and in fact the thin line of demarcation between improvisation and composition is rapidly disappearing.

This process of change does not imply that the blues have disappeared from jazz. They remain a potent fac-

tor, but they have also changed. The blues Bessie Smith
sang were, for the most part, far different from old folk
style blues; yet who would say that "Young Woman's
Blues" is not of the blues line? Part of the power of
Basie's band was due to its rich blues content, although
these are a differently sounding blues from those of the

New Orleans bands. Lester Young's music is saturated in the blues, although here again we have a new and quite different blues music. If we listen carefully to "Dizzy" Gillespie, Charlie Parker and Dexter Gordon it is not hard to find the blues again, transformed. Ellington has made the richest use of the blues throughout his career, from the solos of "Black and Tan Fantasy" to "Cotton Tail," "Across the Track" and "Black, Brown and Beige."

The key to a study of jazz, as of all music, is through its melody. This is not to undervalue the importance of rhythm and harmony in music. Melody, however, implies a rhythm and harmony. If we take a melody like any of those in "High Society" and play it in three-quarter time, the character of the melody is completely lost. If we give it rich and chromatic harmonies, its character again is completely changed. Such experiments, especially harmonic, may lead to the evolution of new melodic lines. The point however is that melodic line, rather than rhythm and harmony, is the key to an analysis of the changing human imagery and emotional content of music. Melody of course, as I have previously pointed out, can be many different things, and is not to be limited to the euphonious, harmonically symmetrical "tune." In the opening movement of the Beethoven Fifth Symphony, for example, the famous four-note opening theme (sometimes called the "Fate" or "Victory" theme, but not by Beethoven) is one kind of melodic phrase. The

development of this theme which follows, playing it
faster and each time repeating it on a higher note, spins
a new kind of melodic line. The "second theme," sweet,
singing and tuneful, is a third kind of melody. Similarly,
in jazz, we have the melody of the blues break, clipped
and concentrated; the melodic line constructed out of a
piling up of repeated phrases, like the King Oliver "Dippermouth" solo or the Picou "High Society" clarinet
solo; the singing, tuneful line, like Dodds' "Lonesome
Blues."

Jazz is an art of melody. Much of this melody consists of the blues, played straight or broken up into small
phrases and rearranged. Some of this melody consists of
folk songs taken from the most varied sources, gathered
up into the general body of jazz, as the spirituals took to
themselves hymn tunes and square dances. In the period
of flourishing New Orleans rag, blues and stomp jazz,
new melodies came from fresh sources; old French
dances that were still part of the city's living music,
Creole songs, minstrel show tunes and dances, songs and
dances of Spanish origin, military and parade marches,
funeral marches, spirituals and hymns, square dances,
even the mock-oriental music often heard in vaudeville.
The jazz musician loved melody. He both improvised
his own melody, and played a familiar melody with deep
affection, adding only the accents and phrasings that any
good artist, folk or professional, adds to a work he performs. The jazz musician often added, to a sweet or non-

blue melody, blue notes, breaks and intonations, thus providing us with a fascinating combination of two musical languages in one. When we understand the dual nature of jazz music, the inseparable opposites that make up the unity of the jazz performance, the hot and sweet, the improvisation and the "straight" performance, the solo and the ensemble, the addition of personal "style" to familiar musical material, we can understand many otherwise inexplicable aspects of jazz.

We can see why so many of the great jazz players, noted for their improvisation, like Joe Oliver, Louis Armstrong, Tommy Ladnier, Johnny Dodds, Ellington and his bandsmen, Kid Ory, so often play close to an original melody, with of course the musical taste, the economy where each note makes its own plangent impact, that marks a creative artist.

We can see that jazz is not simply improvisation on "anything"; that sometimes the difference between an exciting performance and a boring one, by the same fine musicians, is simply due to the fact that the first offered to the musicians good melodic material, the second poor. Thus the latter put a strain on their creative artistry which they weren't always up to. We can understand why so many "evergreens," blues, rags, folk melodies, even pop tunes, come up again and again in the history of jazz, and are still enjoyable today. We can see why, although each jazz player has his own technique and personality, he can also take over bodily and play with affectionate rightness another jazzman's improvisation, as Bechet plays Dodds' "Lonesome Blues" solo, as Williams plays Armstrong's "West End Blues" solo, as Griffin plays Stewart's "Boy Meets Horn," as every jazz clarinet player knows the famous "High Society," "Tiger Rag," "Weary Blues" and "Panama" solos. We can see why the definition of jazz as "pure improvisation" rose only when jazz performances were almost drowned by the flood of hack-created, tin-pan-alley tunes, and the jazz player had to fight his material to make something out of it. We can see why it is possible for a beautiful jazz music to be made out of the popular tune, when the jazz player has assimilated its idioms sufficiently to make it into a strange, free, sinuous and expressive melodic line. Not every popular tune is fit for such treatment, of course, and there is quite a transitional process required. It is the jazz theorist, much more than the player, who has been a "purist."

There is a purity worth fighting for. It is not the purity of a single style or folk material. It is the purity of honest and free musical communication against the manufactured slickness, the repetition and standardization of what were originally living musical ideas, that makes up the vast amount of "popular" music today. However, some theorists lump together as "commercial" everything that appeared in jazz after New Orleans, including in one term the most sensitive and deeply felt creative music and the most uninspired, hack imitations.

They frantically attack the musician for "selling out," which is actually the selfish demand that the musician, at the price of poverty, and also the price of giving up his own right to grow, to experiment with whatever new materials and methods please him, provide the critic with the music that the critic has painfully learned to like.

The point I mentioned above, of one musician playing another's solo or composition, brings up the complicated question of "originality." It is important to remember that there are two diametrically opposed processes. One appears in the cases above, or when Jelly-Roll Morton adapts Oliver's "Chimes Blues," James P. Johnson or Albert Ammons improvises on Pine-top Smith's Boogie-Woogie, Fletcher Henderson makes "Dippermouth" into "Sugarfoot Stomp," Charlie Barnet plays an Ellington composition. It is a process basic to the development of music; of the creative musician, realizing that he is not alone in a musical world, and that he learns only by using, with appreciation, what has gone before. It is an open and honest use of influences, one musician giving credit to another for what he has brought into the musical world. The other is the prevalent tin-pan-alley process, by men with no originality, who take riffs, folk tunes or jazz ideas familiar to every musician, rearrange or embellish them enough to disguise their origin (generally ruining them in the process), and put their name to them as "original compositions."

The entire fetish of "originality," which causes the most creative musicians often to be called "unoriginal" and the greatest fakers to call themselves "original" composers, is a product of commercialism. In a folk culture, music is a common language, as it is indeed in all creative music. The old blues singers used a common stock of melodies and even poetic phrases, familiar as well to their hearers. Their originality lay in the variation, embellishment, personality and fresh character they gave to this common language.

With the rise of the market and the music industry, "originality" became a necessary part of a salable commodity, and so every jazz performance as well as every piece of sheet music had to have a composer's name. Yet, if we examine the popular tunes and band performances of New Orleans, we find them a criss-cross of similarities, repetitions of phrase, re-creations of long existing folk and traditional tunes. Such are many of the tunes used by Joe Oliver, W. C. Handy, Clarence and Spencer Williams, Ferdinand Morton, the members of the Original Dixieland Five.

What happened was that with the rise of the market system, musicians began staking out claims on songs they knew and could rearrange into usable form, like a colonist's staking out claims on virgin land. And, as in the case of the true colonist, the explorer, (not the real-estate sharper who follows when the ground has been cleared) these first music writers and arrangers were pioneers. Their work has the freshness and life of pioneering exploration. They were men of enough creative ability to demand the utmost respect for their work. It is to their credit that they recognized, re-created, put together and built up into a usable form these fine germ melodies; and the pity is that not enough of it was done. These men used the music they knew as a language in which they could speak. They have nothing in common with the plagiarist, who borrows from one man so that he can disguise what he takes from another.

When Brahms was told that his First Symphony showed similarities to Beethoven's Ninth, he replied, "Any fool can see that." The test of originality, in all cases, is musical quality: the taste, inventiveness, and moving quality of the music that is produced, the something old transformed by the something new. This is entirely different from the claim of some jazz enthusiasts that improvisation is all that matters. Jazz, like all music, is a combination of the individual and the social, the inventive craftsmanship and musical thinking with the common body of musical material, each interpenetrating the other. The reason New Orleans music is still so greatly loved today is its wealth of melody, its fresh creation of a living, malleable body of folk lore. It should be, like the folk music of every country, a part of its musicians' and people's consciousness.

A folk music is not a "pure" music. Music taken from many sources becomes part of people's daily lives, their personal and social thinking. Thus used by them, it takes on new characteristics and a new unity whatever its origins. Through such a language we can see how a people live together, how they react to the world and their fellow human beings.

The spirituals were such a music of slavery. Woven out of many sources—African chants, hymn tunes, dances—they expressed not "African memories" but the character and life of the people enslaved. Nor do they represent a flight from reality, a simple hope for a future better life. They are a music of struggle, a struggle carried on within Biblical imagery. They were used in insurrections and as an Underground Railway code. A music like the spirituals is inconceivable as an escape. Only a people who fought slavery, as the Negro people did, with whatever tools they found at hand, would have had the vitality to create so great a music.

Out of the spirituals have come the magnificent body of songs that are now concert pieces. It has become the fashion to decry these present-day spirituals as they are sung by a Paul Robeson or Marian Anderson. They are not the "real thing." Granted that they are not the folk spirituals as actually sung on the plantations, that the real spirituals were a little more free, strange and flexible a music, it is important for us to have this later body of song in our possession. The spirituals are already far behind us, and these songs remain as a crystallization of a great music created by a great people. They have become our heritage, a part of our consciousness. What is important in knowing them is to know their limitations and the society they bring back for us; not to transform into an escape, a music that was originally created for struggle. In parallel fashion, the great compositions of the leaders and members of the New Orleans and Dixieland bands, such as "High Society," "Snag It," "Original Dixieland One-Step," "Fidgety Feet," "Clarinet Marmalade," "Dippermouth Blues," were magnificent concert pieces, created at a time when the body of music from which they came was already slowly becoming a thing of the past. As such, as the crystallizations of a great people's music, they have an undying vitality.

The blues were a music of the semi-feudalism that arose in the South after the sabotage of "Reconstruction." The Negro was tied down, as much as possible, to the land, surrounded by innumerable restrictions. The blues became likewise both a tool and an expression of his struggle for freedom of movement and travel, for freedom of labor, for the decencies of family life. They created new images, drawn from more realistic experience than the Biblical imagery of the spirituals. They spoke of the gambler, the outlaw, the railroad and steamboat, the chain-gang, fire and flood, the labor giant like John Henry, this imagery likewise having a double meaning. They spoke bitterly of man-woman relations, the resentment of the deserted man or of the deserted woman, the assertions of independence. Thus, in a seemingly comic way, a resentment could be expressed against a much more real oppression. The seeming conflicts of sexual life became symbols for the Negro people's resentment at any confinement of their freedom.

The music and verses were of a varied kind. The blues melody I have written above, as a basic blues, was accompanied by a verse like this:

It / rained five days and the / sky turned dark at / night

Three of such lines make up the twelve-bar blues, the second line being generally, in its words, a repetition of the first.

Another form of the blues takes eight, twelve or sixteen bars, and doesn't have the near two-bar breathing space of the form above. A typical verse is the following:

> Work all the Summer, Summer,
> Work all the Fall, Fall,
> Make this Christmas, Christmas,
> Christmas in my overalls.

The music of such blues is sweeter, more diatonic, often in or close to a minor key, using less blue notes. It has a close derivation from hymns, spirituals, mid-West folk songs that originally were transplanted from Europe and underwent strange variations. Typical of such sweet and tender folkish melodies are "How Long, How Long," "When the Sun Goes Down," "Trouble in Mind," "St. James Infirmary." "Careless Love" is another sweet and beautiful folk melody, somewhat different in structure. "South," a favorite of Kansas City bands, is another. In fact many of the blues used by Kansas City bands like Moten's and Basie's are of this sweeter kind, often with a strong jump rhythm. Many of such sweet blues appear in Ellington's early records, such as the opening tunes of "Rocky Mountain Blues," "Big House Blues," "Saturday Night Function," "Rocking in Rhythm," "Saratoga Swing."

Another blues pattern derives directly from the square dance, mountain tune and "breakdown." A typical "breakdown" rhythm pattern is as follows:

> Swing your partners, swing 'em style
> Promenade all and go hog wild.
> Come on, Ida Red!

Similar patterns may easily be recognized in such folk blues as "Stackerlee," in many of the blues sung by Leadbelly, in the blues piano playing and singing of Speckled Red, "Cripple" Clarence Lofton, Montana Taylor, in many jump-rhythm orchestral blues.

New Orleans music was another step forward. It was a music of city life, and the city community; one, moreover, where many musical instruments were available. And so, in using the musical instruments as an extension of the human hand, voice and mind, the character of the blues changed further. They became instrumental, not in the sense of the instrument imitating the voice, which takes place sometimes but is not very important; rather in the sense of the tonal and technical possibilities of the instrument making possible a new blues music. The breaks and riffs, which I have spoken of, are such examples. They are a purely instrumental music, not found in the older, sung blues. They explore the full tonal powers of the instrument. The breaks are a wonderful solo instrument blues. The riffs are a re-creation of the blues in terms of the needs and possibilities of the larger band. When, in later performances such as Louis Armstrong's, we find the voice performing breaks, it is not an example of instrument following voice, but the reverse. The voice is imitating the instrument.

Each step forward towards freedom of the Negro people, and each step forward of their music meant, as well, a vastly enlarged music, both in scope of performance and variety of materials. We find this true in New Orleans music, where new melodic elements far beyond the spirituals and hymn tunes, are absorbed, combining with the blues to bring about a richer folk music, or rather semi-folk, than had ever existed before.

One of the characteristics of New Orleans music, contributing largely to its variety and beauty, is the mixture of different musical languages, the interplay of "hot" and "sweet," blue and non-blue. This fazes the theorists of pure-blues jazz, who either ignore the mixture or assume that the non-blue elements were "subconsciously" assimilated, and immediately "blued," or "Africanized" by the performers. The music indicates otherwise. It reveals, rather, that the interplay of two languages was a most sensitive, highly conscious musical operation, and that it is precisely the artist who is most "folk" (or musically "pure," as the theory goes), who will often also play a non-blue melody straight and with great pleasure in it.

The ragtime piano, often a product of "educated" pianists like Ferdinand "Jelly-Roll" Morton and Lillian Hardin Armstrong, brought many of these "alien" musical contributions to jazz. Morton describes, in his Library of Congress records, the development of a French Quadrille into "Tiger Rag." His "The Crave" shows the Spanish influence, a most prolific one in New Orleans music. The ragtime pianists were great experimenters with idiom, trying out minor-major mixtures and chromatic lines blended with blue or straight diatonic melodies. They often called these experiments a "freakish" music, like the name of one of Morton's own piano solos, or the name of another famous and beautiful rag, "Eccentric." Oliver's "Froggie Moore," Johnny Dodds' and Lil Armstrong's "Goober Dance," Morton's "The Pearls" are typical of such subtle interplay of chromatic and blues figures. The minuet and its associated dances undoubtedly had an important influence on New Orleans music. Ellington's (Bigard) "Minuet in Blues," shows how easily and well the minuet rhythm, syncopated, fits a blues line. If this particular work is explained away as a deliberate "trick" (although the beauty of the music is its own justification), it is still interesting to notice how close the syncopated minuet rhythm parallels many New Orleans rhythmic figures, like the "walking bass," or the "hopscop," with its double-jump, hopping eight-to-the-bar beat. Examples are "New Orleans Hop Scop Blues," "Keystone Blues," "Jazzing Babies Blues," "Organ Grinder Blues," "Bluin' the Blues." Another language influence, giving rise to many chromatic and minor key figures that interplayed with the blues, was that of the mock-oriental, "hoochie-koochie" music. Sidney Bechet's "Egyptian Fantasy" is a fine example of the conscious musical play with this kind of tune and the blues. Other examples are Johnny Dodds' "Oriental Man," Ellington's "Caravan" and the middle theme of his "Rocking in Rhythm." Many favorite New Orleans songs and rags show this influence, like "Shake It and Break It," "Diga-Diga-Doo," "That Da-Da Strain."

Hymn tunes and military marches were absorbed into the New Orleans music, although so complete a fusion took place, this being a living and flexible music, that it is often hard to tell, in a particular case, whether we have an original march given a "blues" treatment, or a folk song given a parade treatment. "High Society" is obviously a march in origin. "Willie the Weeper," "Oh Didn't He Ramble," "Muskat Ramble," are fine folk songs given a march beat. Bunk Johnson's "Maryland My Maryland," Kid Rena's "Gettysburg March," are tunes dating from the past century, given a march form. "When the Saints Go Marching In" is a hymn tune, and "Bucket Got a Hole in It" is a similar hymnal tune. Another hymn-like tune is Johnny Dodds' beautiful "Gate Mouth," which is also heard, note for note, in Kid Rena's "Get it Right." Creole songs played an important part in the idiom of New Orleans jazz. The rightness with which many of Kid Ory's performances of Creole songs fit into the jazz framework indicates that many of the well-loved New Orleans tunes were Creole in origin.

New Orleans music is a rich body of song, of grand, moving, luxuriant melody. New Orleans music, considered only as a "style," is almost meaningless. It is a music. The difference between "New Orleans" and "Dixieland" music may be explained somewhat in these terms. "New Orleans" was a people's music, free, varied, constantly changing and experimental. "Dixieland" is a style and a repertory made up of this music, narrower in content and almost rigidly fixed in its phrasing, instrumentation and performance. To listen to a Dixieland jazz session today is almost like listening to a classical concert. It is a very precious and worthwhile experience, like Szigeti playing the Beethoven concerto and Horowitz playing Chopin. It is far from what the full art of jazz should be and is, just as a concert of nineteenth century music is far from what the full art of music should be and is in our time. And this is true even though Szigeti perhaps plays the Beethoven concerto better than any violinist of Beethoven's day, Horowitz may play better than Chopin himself did, and a first-class Dixieland group probably plays with more finesse, subtlety and beauty of tone than the average New Orleans group of musicians.

The mixture, absorption and highly conscious interplay of many musical languages is not accidental to New Orleans music but the key to understanding it, just as it is also the key to understanding the entire growth of jazz since that time. Such an interplay is taking place today, in bebop, although the languages involved are quite different. It should interest the musical student to discover how much such an interplay of language is a part of the entire history of music, folk and composed. One of the greatest examples came when Martin Luther adopted a body of folk songs, Gregorian chants, and other musical elements into the body of the Lutheran chorale, or hymnology, giving Protestant composers a basic language for them to expand upon. Bach's "St. Matthew Passion" and organ chorale preludes provide a wonderful example of this great composer's use of these chorales, performing them "straight" and also playing with them against other languages, folk or chromatic and dissonant. The rondos of the Mozart concertos and chamber works are full of examples of his using a folk dance, or horn call, and playing it against other more sophisticated idioms. Beethoven will often start a work—the most famous example is the Fifth Symphony—by teasing the audience with a "major" feeling, before he moves into the true "minor" upon which the movement is based.

Because New Orleans music was so fertile in melody, out of it came the great wealth of American popular song of the 1910's and 1920's. We have here an interesting case of a music predominantly vocal, the blues and other folk song bodies, giving rise to a music predominantly instrumental, that of New Orleans slow drags, rags and stomps, and that, in turn, giving rise to a new vocal music, the thirty-two bar "ragtime" song, often with a rich blues feeling. Out of this music came a great mass of popular songs, some good and some bad; the bad ones mainly due to the market-place system, which demanded a continual "novelty" faster than good songs could be invented, and caused the song concocter to arise. "Alexander's Ragtime Band" might have been born out of "There'll Be a Hot Time in the Old Town Tonight." "Squeeze Me" is an old blues which may be heard under many names, such as "Boy in the Boat." "Stormy Weather" is a product of blues improvisation, heard in the opening measures of Oliver's "West End Blues," Teagarden's blue solo in "That's a Serious Thing," Pecora's solo in "Reincarnation." "Basin Street Blues" and "Georgia on My Mind" are cousins. "Old Man River" is based on a common blues riff, heard in Oliver's "Canal Street Blues" and even more recognizably in Clarence Williams' "Royal Garden Blues." "Sister Kate" is close to "Bailin' the Jack." "Summertime" is close to Handy's "St. Louis Blues," which itself combines, as Handy himself explains, Spanish themes and basic blues. "I Can't Give You Anything But Love," the anti-bar-line character of which Winthrop Sargeant dissects in his "Jazz, Hot and Hybrid," is in part a slow version of "Twelfth Street Rag," a fact which would help to explain better the point Sargeant makes.

These derivations, of course, are not pointed out in the spirit of a "tune detective." Such continuity is characteristic of the entire art of music. The value of New Orleans music to us, and to music history is, first, that it is in itself so great a body of music and, second, that it, and through it the Negro people, gave the American people so wonderful a treasure of beloved song.

RECORD ILLUSTRATIONS—CHAPTER THREE

Spirituals—Hymn Tune Style

SISTER B. PHILLIPS AND HAROLD LEWIS
God Leads His Dear Children Along (Circle 3001)

SISTER ERNESTINE WASHINGTON
The Lord Will Make a Way Somehow, Does Jesus Care (Disc 710)

HUDDLE LEADBETTER (LEADBELLY)
We Shall Walk Through the Valley (in Disc. Album 660)

Also ROSETTA THARPE record listed in Chap. 2

Spirituals—Archaic Folk Style

MITCHELL CHRISTIAN SINGERS
I'm Praying Humble, The Saints are Marching (Columbia Reissue); Walk With Me, The Bridegroom's Coming (Columbia 37483)

LEADBELLY
Talking, Preaching (in Disc Album 660)

Spirituals—Solo Song and Concert Style

MARION ANDERSON
Hold On, Poor Me (Victor 10-1278)

ROLAND HAYES
Were You There, Hear The Lambs A' Cryin (Columbia 69812)

PAUL ROBESON with LAWRENCE BROWN
Eight Spirituals (Columbia Album 610)

Blues—Basic Twelve Bar

BESSIE SMITH
Lost Your Head Blues (Columbia 35674)

MA RAINEY
Black Dust Blues (Paramount Reissue 12926)

HOCIEL THOMAS
Go Down Sunshine (Circle 1014)

MEMPHIS MINNIE
It Was You, Baby (Columbia 37462)

FERDINAND "JELLY-ROLL" MORTON
Mamie's Blues (Commodore 4001)

COOT GRANT
Evil Gal Blues (King Jazz 147)

SONNY TERRY
Harmonica Blues (Columbia 37686)

EDITH JOHNSON
Good Chib Blues, and COW COW DAVENPORT—Jim
Crow Blues (Paramount, Reissued on Century 3021)

MEADE LUX LEWIS
Whistle Blues (Blue Note 39)

*Blues—Folk Song, Hymn Tune, Work Song, Breakdown and
Dance Patterns*

BESSIE SMITH
New Orleans Hop Scop Blues (Columbia 37577)

BERTHA HILL
Careless Love, Trouble in Mind (Circle 1004)

JACK DUPREE
Dupree Shake Dance (Columbia 37335)

LEADBELLY
Negro Work Songs, Country Dances, etc. (in Disc Album 660)

MEMPHIS MINNIE
I'm Not a Bad Gal (Columbia 37562)

JOE WILLIAMS
Stack of Dollars (Columbia 38055)

SONNY TERRY AND OH RED
Harmonica and Washboard Breakdown (Columbia 37686)

FERDINAND MORTON
Wining Boy Blues, Buddy Bolden Blues, Don't You Leave Me
Here (Commodore 4004,3,5)

BILL GAITHER (LEROY'S BUDDY)
How Long, Baby, How Long and After the Sun Goes Down
(Decca 48044)

MA RAINEY
Leavin' This Morning (Paramount Reissue 12902)

Twelve Bar Blues—Instrumental

LOUIS ARMSTRONG AND BAND
S.O.L. Blues (Columbia 35661)

DEWEY JACKSON'S PEACOCK ORCHESTRA
Capitol Blues (Brunswick 1010)

ART HODES AND HIS CHICAGOANS
Slow 'Em Down Blues (Blue Note 506)

KID ORY'S CREOLE JAZZ BAND
Blues for Jimmy (Crescent-2)

BUNK JOHNSON AND HIS NEW ORLEANS BAND
Franklin St. Blues (Victor 40-0129) Snag It (Victor 40-0126)
*(See also fine performances of "Snag It" by King Oliver—Bruns-
wick 1010—Kid Ory—Circle 12001—Muggsy Spanier—Commodore 616)*

BABY DODDS TRIO, WITH ALBERT NICHOLAS
Albert's Blues (Circle 1002)

KID RENA'S DELTA JAZZ BAND
Lowdown Blues (Circle 1035)

LOUIS ARMSTRONG
   Gutbucket Blues (Columbia 36152)

Blues Treatment of Hymns, Creole, and other Traditional New Orleans Songs

KID ORY'S CREOLE JAZZ BAND
   Bucket Got a Hole in It, Eh La Bas, Creole Bo Bo, Joshua Fought the Battle of Jericho (in Columbia Album 126)

KID RENA'S DELTA JAZZ BAND
   Get in Right (Circle 1038)

BABY DODDS JAZZ FOUR
   Winin' Boy Blues, Careless Love (Blue Note 518)

JACK TEAGARDEN'S BIG EIGHT
   St. James Infirmary (HRS 2006)

ECLIPSE ALLEY FIVE
   Bucket Got a Hole in It (Circle 1612)

BUNK JOHNSON'S NEW ORLEANS BAND
   My Maryland, Tishimongo Blues (Decca 35132, 1) When The Saints Go Marching In (Victor 40-0126)

"RED" ALLEN AND ORCHESTRA
   Canal Street Blues (Decca 19092)

LOUIS ARMSTRONG AND ORCHESTRA
   Down in Honky Tonk (Decca 18091)

LU WATTERS YERBA BUENA BAND
   Working Man Blues (West Coast 104)
   (King Oliver's original performance of this work may be available on Hot Jazz Club of America—7)

The Break

LOUIS ARMSTRONG AND BAND
   Cornet Chop Suey (Columbia 36154) Potato Head Blues (Columbia 35660) Oriental Strut, You're Next (Columbia 35660) Wild Man Blues (Brunswick 80059)

JOHNNY DODDS AND ORCHESTRA
Come on and Stomp, Stomp, Stomp (Brunswick 80074)

BECHET-SPANIER BIG FOUR
If I Could Be With You (HRS 2002)
(For interesting treatments of the break, see "Snag It" recordings, and "Joe Turner Blues," "One and Two Blues," "Skid-Dat-De-Dat," "Bragging in Brass," "Congo Blues" in listings above and in Chapter 2)

The Riff, Early Style

LOUIS ARMSTRONG AND ORCHESTRA
Savoy Blues (Columbia 37537)

JOHNNY DODDS AND ORCHESTRA
Red Onion Blues, Gravier St. Blues (Decca 18094)

FERDINAND MORTON
King Porter Stomp (Commodore 4005)

ART HODES
A Selection from the Gutter, Organ Grinder Blues (Commodore 545)

LOUIS ARMSTRONG AND ORCHESTRA
2:19 Blues (Decca 18090)

It was the W.P.A. of the 1930's that inaugurated the large scale study of American folk music, led by men like John A. Lomax and Benjamin A. Botkin. Unfortunately the magnificent Library of Congress recordings that resulted are insufficiently available for knowledge and study. The transformation in appreciation of our folk lore, however, is a permanent one, and is seen in the work being done by Alan Lomax for Decca, George Avakian for Columbia, Moe Asch for Disc.

It is a disgrace that a great mass of the most beautiful music ever created in America is still locked away in the files of the commercial record companies. Some of Bessie Smith's finest "straight" blues, like "Backwater Blues" with its dramatic flood story, "Poor Man Blues" with its protest against mistreatment, are out of print, as well as records by other singers such as Leroy Carr, Ma Rainey, Bessie Tucker, who exhibit the untrained human voice in all its flexibility of expression, making its own music and poetry. A careful sifting of the records, issued by the companies originally, with typical snobbery, as "race records," would unearth a few hundred of the utmost value in studying American history, American music, and the origins of all music. Blues records are still being made. They exhibit generally, however, the mentality of the manufacturer rather than the fluid, changing and creative words and music of people making their own art for their own social needs.

Among the songs listed here as "Spirituals, Concert Style," it is interesting to pick out their varied origins. Most of them, like "Bye and Bye," "Go Down Moses," "Hold On," are clearly antiphonal in structure. "Balm in Gilead" is a fine hymn-like tune. "Sometimes I Feel" and "Were You There" are close to the blues. "Jericho" is typical of the revival meeting and the "jump" rhythm.

The origin of the songs listed as folk song and dance blues, and traditional New Orleans songs, is anybody's guess, and the ear is the most important judge. Songs undergo strange transformations in use. The popular hit of a few years back, "Pistol Packing Momma," is almost note for note a Creole song, and many a hymn tune has been put to secular use, reversing the process whereby hymn tunes were originally made out of secular songs.

CHAPTER FOUR

IMPROVISATION AND JAZZ FORM

The first definition of jazz to be widely accepted was "collective improvisation." If the question rose, "Improvisation on what?" the answer given was "on anything."

A deeper study of jazz revealed the paramount importance of the blues to jazz, not as simply a special body of the music but permeating its fabric. It was also recognized that jazz had many aspects of a folk music. This is as far as many theorists have gone. Jazz remains "collective improvisation," and as such, it is "formless." It has no relation to the world history of music other than being different. To some who take their theories from the surrealist art and poetry of the 1920's, jazz is the music of the "subconscious" or "unconscious." To others, taking their theories from a flimsy understanding of the futurist painting of the '20's, it is the "music of the future," which will replace all composition and form as outmoded institutions.

The truth is not quite so startling. Jazz is largely improvisation, but the division between improvisation and composition is not as drastic as believed, nor is jazz so completely different from all other world music as to exist wholly by its own invented laws. Jazz follows old and familiar patterns of music, and is new only in that it follows these patterns in terms of its own rhythms, melodies and timbres.

Improvisation is a form of composition. Improvisation is music that is not written down, composition is music that is written down. The difference is very important. The ability to write music makes possible a bigness of form and richness of expression that is beyond the limits of improvisation. It is a great advantage to be able to plan a major, complex work, and spend many months on working out its structure and details. It is an advantage to have such forms as opera, sonata and symphony, granted that the cultural life of the times makes it possible for the composer to put living human images into them. These forms make possible a treatment in music of broad dramatic and psychological experiences that are necessary to a full cultural life. This difference, the extension of forms and expressive possibilities, is the real difference between improvisation and composition, not the fact that improvisation is "alive" and composition is "dead" or mechanical. The latter charge is frequently justified, but only because of the "dead man" attitude that marks much classical and composed music today. A work of composed music, properly performed, should sound as alive as if it were being improvised.

Improvisation was always a basic method of folk art. And it continued into the most advanced forms of musical composition, such as concerto and opera, up to the nineteenth century, when the drastic separation was finally established between the performer and composer. Handel, in the early eighteenth century, wrote his organ concertos with many "ad lib" directions, and all his composed work showed an almost improvisational flexibility. J. M. Coopersmith points out, in his edition of "The Messiah," [1] for example, that the same aria was written by Handel in six different versions, ranging from a soprano solo to a duet for two contraltos with chorus; each version, like the several versions of a hot solo, as "right" as the other. Handel, J. S. Bach, Mozart, Beethoven, were famous improvisors, and while we have no record of their improvisations, there is every reason to believe that similar material was incorporated into their compositions.

If we examine carefully what happens in jazz improvisation, we see that it is really a kind of composition. It is the height of superficiality to imagine that a hot solo

[1] Carl Fischer, New York, 1947.

emerges directly from a performer's "unconscious." People simply cannot create on a consistent level this way. A great hot solo is generally worked up from performance to performance, using the same material. If we follow the work of a jazz performer, we can trace the growth of these solos. When the player arrives at a creation that satisfies him, he remembers it and repeats it. At a jam session of high quality, some solos are new and some old, although the spirit of the occasion, the contagion of the performance, makes them all sound fresh and new. A group of Dixieland players will often do a familiar "evergreen" with almost all the nuances of a previous performance.

To say this is not to detract from the jazz player's originality, but merely to point out the conditions under which every creative mind works. The slow creation of a great jazz solo is a form of musical composition. If improvisation sounds to us more alive and contagious, it is because a fine improvisation is much more exciting than bad composed music, or even good, played by uninterested performers. Hot jazz improvisors are careful workmen and fine craftsmen; they generally know what they are doing every step of the way. Jazz improvisors are inspired by each other's solos, but composers are also stimulated by hearing other composers' music.

Improvisation is a basic characteristic of jazz, but jazz musicians are not a new kind of genius who pour forth music upon any provocation like water from Moses' rock. The mediocre quality and dullness of the music that frequently results from "all-star combinations," brought together for recording purposes, is due to the theory that places all its belief in the mystical "improvisational genius," and forgets the need for musical material and a common language. Many jazz musicians are phenomenal musical thinkers. Their improvisation, however, like "genius," is a product of infinite pains, of the slow germination and maturity of musical ideas.

When we understand jazz improvisation, as a process of unwritten composition consciously worked out and carefully built up from performance to performance, much then becomes clear about jazz that is otherwise a mystery. We can see why it is impossible to ask that a performance be wholly invented on the spur of the moment, wholly fresh and different in every phrase. A great improvised performance must necessarily be a combination of old and new, familiar and fresh material. If half of what is heard is truly new, the performance is miraculous. We can see why a group of the very finest performers generally do better with a familiar number than with a wholly fresh melody. They know all the nuances, the ins and outs of the old piece. They have worked it out many times, and have a base from which to go further. A fresh number is generally approached gingerly, played "straight" until its possibilities begin to be felt out. We can see, on the other hand, why so many performances by second-rate swing bands where every-

body seems to be improvising at white heat, sound abys-
mally dull. The reason is that the soloists, having made
their bow to the starting tune, proceed to knock out the
same hot solos they performed twenty times before to
twenty other numbers; solos that in many cases are only
a noodling of chords with a hot attack and intonation.
This aimless swing, all "style" and no melody, springs
from the fallacy that "improvisation" is everything, and
the material worked with doesn't matter. The poorer the
material, the more the solos themselves tend to fall into
dull, standardized patterns.

This leads us to a most important point to remember
about improvisation. It is not only method, but matter.
It requires not only the ability to invent, but a language
in which to invent. If the average classical musician of
today were asked to improvise, he would be at a loss.
In the eighteenth century, however, the average performing musician would improvise very willingly, just as he
could also turn out a respectable composed piece. What
happens today in classical music, unlike jazz, is that the
average conservatory graduate thinks of music in terms
of a past language, one completely set and contained
within the masterpieces or semi-masterpieces he performs.
He can love the music of Mozart, Beethoven and Brahms
but not improvise in that language, except as a clever but
artistically worthless reshuffling of their music. To improvise successfully he must have a musical language that
has become part of his thought processes. The blues and

rags are such a language to the hot jazz musician, as are other forms of folk and popular music when they become part of his musical thinking. The jazz improvisor's mind is well stocked with musical phrases capable of countless variation and formation into new patterns.

An insight into the process of improvisation can be gotten from a description of one of the oldest and most widespread of improvised arts, that of acting. The "Commedia della Arte," the "Italian Comedy" which flourished throughout Europe for three centuries, the sixteenth through the eighteenth, was a theatre of improvisation, building up countless new dramatic and comic patterns out of stock, masked figures such as Harlequin, Columbine, Pantaloon, Scaramouche, and others. It was a most important art form in Europe, influencing opera, written drama and even painting. A description of the improvising actor, written by a contemporary, reads like a perfect description of the art of a jazz musician.

"For a good Italian actor is a man of infinite resources and resourcefulness . . . he matches his words and actions so perfectly with those of his colleagues on the stage that he enters instantly into whatever acting and movements are required of him in such a manner as to give the impression that all that they do has been prearranged.[1]

But all this improvisation rose from a memory base.

[1] Pierre Louis Duchartre, *The Italian Comedy,* London, George C. Harap, Ltd., 1929, p. 31.

"Certain it is that there never was such a thing as complete and absolute improvisation, nor ever can be. . . . his (Barbieri's) memory was stored with phrases, concetti (conceits), declarations of love, reproaches, delirium and despairs."

It may sound paradoxical, but it is true that only because this body of musical language exists can hot jazz continue to be so fresh and inventive. One is impossible without the other. A performer, in a jam session, could not carry on so well from a previous performer's solo, did he not speak the same musical language. In the two and three-voice improvised ensembles of New Orleans jazz, what we generally hear is basic blues line from trumpet, clarinet and trombone. One little fresh nuance from any instrument is enough to make the entire ensemble take on vibrancy and life. One new phrase, or old phrase in a new combination, is enough to transform the entire musical texture. It is because the jazz improvisor has so familiar a base to rise from that he can soar.

The blues are particularly adapted to improvisation because even the shortest blues phrase is a self-contained melodic phrase. This phrase can be built up into ever new combinations, like blocks of stone in an arch, and a continually fresh and interesting music made out of the simplest elements.

The construction of a hot jazz solo brings a considerable element of musical form into jazz. For a good hot solo is a musical structure. It follows the laws of all music of quality. The Oliver "Dippermouth" solo is built out of the repetitions of short germ phrases, as Schubert builds a song out of the repetitions of a few phrases, or as Beethoven, on a much larger scale, handles the four-note theme of his Fifth Symphony. All outstanding hot solos are similar constructions, such as that of Joe Smith in "Stampede," Coleman Hawkins in "Hello, Lola," the traditional Picou solo in "High Society," Louis Armstrong in "Mahogany Hall Stomp," Lester Young in "Slow Drag." These solos have a perfect economy of material, and logic in putting their phrases together.

When a popular tune is "blued," it is broken down into fragments, which are turned into blues phrases, and these made the basis for a new musical structure. A fine hot solo on a popular tune, like Louis Armstrong's "I Can't Give You Anything But Love" and "Squeeze Me," Bix Beiderbecke's "Way Down Yonder in New Orleans," Lester Young's "Lady be Good" and "Indiana," Jack Teagarden's "Dinah," is simpler in the basic phrases it uses than the pop tune itself, yet far more complex, well constructed and interesting a musical composition.

Some of the outstanding performers, hailed as great improvisors, base their power on nothing more than a solid blues melody and phrase. This is pointed out not to detract from the originality of these players, but to define the character of their music. Johnny Dodds was a very great jazz performer, playing an almost pure blues, and George Brunis makes his Dixieland performance so exciting precisely because he plays so unvaried a blues and tailgate trombone style.

Another characteristic of the blues, lending themselves to fine improvisation, is their dual, antiphonal character, their "statement and answer," giving the jazz performer the opportunity for the most subtle opposition of rhythmic figures, and for a soaring flight of melody followed by a "return home." Out of this antiphonal pattern of the blues rises the exciting delayed attack, so characteristic of the "hot style." It is really an underlining of the presence of two opposing rhythmic patterns.

Out of it also comes the basic character of the jazz "collective ensemble." This is not, generally, a simultaneous soaring by all the instruments, but a subtle interplay of statement and answer. The ensembles of the King Oliver Creole Band records, with Johnny Dodds playing against the trumpet line of Oliver and Armstrong, are particularly beautiful examples, as are many of Sidney Bechet's final ensembles, against a trumpet player of the calibre of Tommy Ladnier, Muggsy Spanier, Bill ·Davison and Max Kaminsky. Out of this duet form of improvisation comes the elaboration of the "chase," familiar in bebop and riff music. Out of the statement-and-answer pattern comes the tight, unified musical form found in so many fine jazz performances. It is not to be described as a "theme and variations," a form sometimes found in later attempts at "sweet swing" music. It is a much more subtle music of a continual flow and interweaving of melodic lines, repetition and contrast of melodic phrase. In many New Orleans and Ellington performances, it is impossible to tell where one "variation" ends and another begins. The same characteristic recurs in bebop. "Round about Midnight" by Theolonius Monk, for example, is built on the twelve-bar, antiphonal blues pattern, and we can trace the statement and answer, the downward and upward curve of blues melody, although it is hidden in an elaborate harmonic and instrumental texture.

If we study the antiphonal, duet character of the blues melodic line, we will see that it carries over into the hot solo itself. This may seem paradoxical, but if we examine the many great blues solos of jazz, such as those of Louis Armstrong, Johnny Dodds, and Sidney Bechet, we will find two contrasting melodic lines laid down within the same solo, as if the one instrument were playing both the melodic lead and the accompaniment or decoration, the riff and the break. Armstrong and Dodds, in "Wild Man Blues," "Gully Low Blues" ("S. O. L. Blues"), provide fine examples, as do also Dodds' "Lonesome Blues" solo, Armstrong's "Melancholy Blues," "West End Blues," "Basin Street Blues." Lester Young's solos are often of this character, using the low, honking tones of the tenor sax to lay down the contrasting, bass melodic line. J. C. Higginbotham built up a similar brilliant solo style on the trombone, taking over many of Armstrong's trumpet figures.

It is worth noticing that this creation of two contrasting melodic voices by the one instrument is exactly the principle which J. S. Bach uses in his suites and sonatas for unaccompanied violin, cello or flute, and in the writing for solo instrument in his concertos, employing organ-point and arpeggio.

Another characteristic of the blues, making for rich improvisational possibilities, is their non-diatonic character. The traditional chords used to accompany the blues are not determining factors of blues melody, but act rather as punctuation marks, commas or periods, in between which and against which the melodic lines can move with the widest latitude, striking off any kind of apparent dissonance.

This combination of a simple, familiar melodic, rhythmic and harmonic base, with a free range of movement, makes possible the ensemble and collective improvisation, so wonderful in New Orleans jazz. Every performer knows where he has to be, harmonically and melodically, at the right time. Every performer knows the same blues language, the restriction he must accept, and the latitude permitted him. Thus, in what seems to be and, of course, is, a free collective improvisation, each performer will actually be playing the blues; one its rapid, repeated, lead phrases, another its long held notes or slow-moving lines with off-beat accents, a third its inversions. In later swing jazz, such as that of Red Nichols and Benny Goodman, this quality tended to be lost, for the blues were no longer a familiar language to the players, and the solos tended to be bound by the under-lying, "sweet" chords. In Ellington and modern jazz, such as bebop, the free harmonic and improvisational character return, as in the blues, but much different. The blues and jazz music have in the meantime gotten an education.

A last characteristic of the blues, making for suc-cessful improvisation, is that they are a language familiar to both performers and audience. The performers do not merely "express themselves," but communicate to their listeners. Jazz improvisation reaches its greatest heights when its language is shared by both performers and listeners, so that the most subtle variation and twist of phrase immediately makes its impact on the mind; so that even when the audience is dancing, the melodic and rhythmic patterns will translate themselves into dance moods and dance patterns.

That jazz music speaks almost as if its melodic phrases and intonations were words may seem to make for a strange music, to those whose musical experiences are wrapped up in the concert-hall. This is not however a "secret" language that jazz is speaking. All music is meant to speak freshly and directly to the listener, as jazz does to those who know its language. Music in the past spoke sharply to its listeners, as we know from some of the reactions of listeners. A Beethoven dissonance, or a Mozart folk theme, was meant to affect the listeners of its time as it did, with a recognizable change of emotional connotation or human imagery. It is only in our present concert-hall atmosphere that all music is transformed into an escape to a romantic past world, and all musical languages become amalgamated into one dreamy sweetness. In its "speaking" quality jazz is not bringing an unheard-of quality to music, nor is it an example, as some would describe it, of a folkish quaintness. It is a restoration to music of a necessary quality, temporarily abandoned in our "classical" musical atmosphere.

Jazz improvisation, far from being opposed to "form," is inseparable from jazz form. And jazz form is inseparable from the role of jazz as a social art.

In describing the hot solo, I have already indicated the entrance in jazz of an element of form, comparable to composed music. Other aspects of form as well are found in jazz.

One aspect of form in music is the general construction, or layout of a work, fitting it to a definite use, a setting and an audience. Another aspect is the unity and coherence of a work of music, its organization so that it has a recognizable beginning, middle and end, and the entire work makes a single impact. Both of these elements of form are found in jazz, although not to the same degree of expansion and complexity found in the more ambitious composed music. However, many jazz blues and song forms are as perfect pieces of musical structure as art songs by Schubert or Mussorgsky, and many instrumental blues, rags and stomps are as perfectly organized as dances and marches by Handel, Bach, Mozart, Schubert or other masters.

The folk twelve-bar blues is a perfect art form. It may seem to repeat the same musical phrases over and over again, but this is because variety of the form is provided in the words, the poetry. The blues singer, like the ancient troubadour, was often a wandering ballad singer, and his song told a story, frequently in language of great beauty, wit and imagination. Contrary to the beliefs of some esthetes, who blame the "masses" for the idiocy prevalent in manufactured popular art, it is natural for people to prefer words and music that have meaning to them, that have realistic images, laughter and sadness, satire and serious story. A verse like the following is fine poetry, in its honesty, and joyous feeling for reality.

> Work-day—day's a breaking
> Peas in the pot and hoe-cake's baking
> Green corn, come along Charlie . . .

The sung blues often attained as well a fine, if still simple, musical form. The second line would repeat the first but the melody would change; the third line of words would be different, but the melody would end up as in the beginning. This provided a fine unity and variety, built on an interplay of words and music. The instrumental accompaniment added a formal element of variation and repetition, and a three-voice melody, obbligato and bass texture, similar to, if far simpler than, the "trio" linear texture of the Bach arias and instrumental sonatas.

With the rise of instrumental jazz, the accompaniment to the blues became increasingly subtle and elaborate, creating a powerfully organized musical form. Louis Armstrong's blues accompaniments are fine examples, often starting with a simple phrase, like the mocking repetition of a single note in "Cold in Hand" and "You've Been a Good Old Wagon"; then flowering out in increasingly broad phrases, rising to a climax in a full solo chorus, closing with a sweet cadence, "tag" or break. Joe Smith also beautifully organized his blues accompaniments to Bessie Smith's performances, supporting the voice harmonically more than Louis. In "Hard Driving Papa" he creates a most beautiful piece of music, against Bessie's fine, straight twelve-bar blues, by a series of breaks throughout the record, each starting on the same note.

Blues piano, popularly known as "boogie-woogie," provides examples of perfectly organized musical form. It is a genuine three voice music. Vocal records, such as "Roll 'em Pete" by Pete Johnson and Joe Turner, "Head Rag Hop" by Romeo Nelson, Pinetop Smith's "Pinetop Blues," Montana Taylor's "In the Bottom," Meade Lux Lewis' "Blues Whistle" show clearly the relation of the sung blues to the upper and lower piano lines, and enable us to hear more clearly the beautiful re-creation of these three voices in terms of the piano alone. An important element of the formal organization of blues piano was the use of a kind of registration, the adroit contrasting of tone colors between the lower, middle and upper registers of the instrument, often using the brilliant upper register for a climax. The left hand provides not only a rhythm and simple harmony, as in rag piano, but a rolling, blues figure, which gives the music a solid foundation, produces the most interesting dissonances between right and left hand blues lines. The right hand provides the blues statement and answer; the melody and the decorative, answering and pictorially illustrative figures. One of the finest blues piano works, in simple folk style, is Pine-top Smith's "Pinetop's Boogie Woogie." Jim Yancey shows a similar poignant simplicity, as in "Boodlin'" ("Slow and Easy Blues"), but also builds up magnificent, complex compositions by varying his left hand as well as the right, and making the music move through a subtle, off-beat interplay of right and left hand. "Eternal Blues," "Yancey Stomp" and "How Long, How Long Blues" are among his masterpieces. Meade Lux Lewis is a master of intricate right hand work, mixing blues figures, riffs, trills, tremolos and guitar-like arpeggios in the colorful railroad music of "Honky-Tonk Train," and "Chicago Flyer." He also plays a subtle and harmonically inventive slow blues. Pete Johnson is fine in the engaging lightness of his right hand figures, and in the tender, singing character of his sweeter Kansas-City style blues, which he always develops through sharp dynamic contrasts between one phrase and the next. Albert Ammons uses driving, riff-like figures in the right hand as well as the left, building up a powerfully intense and sonorous music. "Cripple" Clarence Lofton uses, by contrast, a simple, jump-like left hand and brilliant, dancing off-beat right hand figures.

All of this music translates into piano timbres the fullness of blues jazz; voice, orchestra, solo instrument, answering accompaniment, musical illustration and rhythm. Blues piano has given us a body of musical composition which stands up, in its own right, as music, with or without the "folk" label. No composer's art could improve on the repeated, rolling figures with which Lewis closes out "Honky-Tonk Train," the break climax of "Yancey Stomp" and the riffing with which it ends, the passacaglia-like variations of "How Long, How Long," the subtle variations and repetitions of "Eternal Blues" and Art Hodes' "A Melody From the Gutter"; the bitter sweet contrasts of Pete Johnson's "Pete's Blues" and Lewis' "Blues, Part Two."

Blues piano form did not rise in the privacy of a composer's room. It was a product of the social use to which the music was put. The piano, played in poor man's saloons and dances, or in Chicago rent parties, had to carry in itself the full burden of dance and song. This burden gave the blues pianist a musical problem to solve, and out of his solution, exploiting for the purpose the full resources of the instrument, the massive forms of boogie-woogie piano took shape.

New Orleans jazz was prolific in musical forms because music filled so many social and communal roles in the city's life. Some of these forms were the "honky-tonk" piano rags; the slow dances and fast dances, or stomps, arranged out of the blues; the marching jazz; the sixteen-bar, popular ragtime song; the combination of all the above, used for funerals, weddings, celebrations, and almost every aspect of the city life of the Negro people. It was truly a people's music, in form and content. In fact the form and content, the social role the music played and the human feelings within it, are indistinguishable. It was also the music of an exploited, poverty-stricken and jim-crowed people. These are the two contrasting truths that must be remembered. It was a social, communal, people's music, and it was a ghetto music. These contradictions known, we can understand why the music had such power, and why the musicians eventually felt dissatisfied with its limitations.

The piano rags touched the two extremes of New Orleans life. As an "educated" music, often produced by pianists who had taken lessons, they have a content of minuet, quadrille and other forms of taught music. At the same time, they were heard in the brothels, which were a subtle form of exploitation and discrimination against the Negro people, since it was only by that sort of entertainment of white people that many Negroes could make a living.

The brothel background has given rise to lurid versions of New Orleans jazz, and some fanciful theories. Its influence on the music, however, is negligible, except in that here was a place where a rag pianist could earn a few dollars. Far more deep-rooted influences on New

Orleans music were the parades, river-boats and social dances. The rags were a great influence on New Orleans music, but largely for their "educated" background. From the piano rags, jazz got an instrumental virtuosity that had been lacking in the folk blues. It is not hard to see a translation of the glittering runs and decorative figures of the ragtime piano in the dancing clarinet decorations of New Orleans band music. Another gift of the piano rags was a more complex and organized musical design. They contributed a sixteen-bar theme, contrasting to and enriching the twelve-bar blues theme. They provided a music built upon the contrast of two distinct themes, one serving as a refrain, the other for development and variation; a form similar to the "rondo" of classical music, which also, incidentally, originated in old European folk dance. They provided a recognition of key, or a diatonic music, with an accompanying ability to modulate, or change key. Almost every piece of New Orleans marching jazz has such a modulation. The simple harmonies of ragtime piano provided a base for standardizing the instrumental ensembles of band music, and thus making possible the interplay of solo and ensemble, of diatonic and non-diatonic language, that is an essential quality of New Orleans music. Contrary to those theories which hold that New Orleans music came wholly from the "unconscious," is the fact that arrangements, the skeleton outline of harmonies and ensembles, played a prominent role in this music. Examples are the work of Lil Armstrong for King Oliver's band, and that of Ferdinand Morton for all the groups with which he recorded.

Thus it was largely out of the marriage of rags and blues that the great New Orleans music flowered, with the additional fertilization of hymns, spirituals, folk songs of every origin, marches, cake-walks and other folk dances. The blues provided the wonderfully poignant melodies; the non-diatonic musical language, and the soaring freedom that resulted from it. They permeated the musical form and provided the most subtle contrasts of "hot" and "sweet," of blue and non-blue idiom. The blues provided the riffs and breaks so important to the new jazz forms. They provided finally the essential antiphonal character, the statement and answer, the forward movement through a constant series of contrasts and surprises, the "heart-beat," which is so moving and human a quality of the music. The rags provided the impulse towards a greater technical mastery of the instrument, the brilliant runs and decorative figures, the interplay and contrast of themes, the use of "key." Out of the two, blues and rags, rose a music of the most finely organized form.

This form made an adroit use of instrumental timbre. The clarinet, trumpet and trombone were a perfect combination, each different in range and in its musical role so that simply by each following out its natural kind of movement, a most rich ensemble and contrast of solo could be created. This was a phenomenon similar to the rise of polyphonic music in European folk music, where the contrasting voices of tenor, alto and bass, each starting with the same melody but following its own natural line of movement, brought into being a beautiful, if rough, polyphonic music. One of the most enjoyable aspects of New Orleans music is the use of contrasting of timbres of the instruments, for variation and climax, not only in ensembles but in the manner with which a driving, full ensemble is followed by the voice of the solo clarinet, the clarinet by the rough, staccato voice of the trumpet or trombone, and so on to the final, climactic ensemble or ride-out. A fine use is also made of the blues language; solos often start relatively sweet, and then become progressively hotter, more blue, wider in their instrumental range. Kid Rena's "Lowdown Blues" is a fine example of such construction.

A most important principle of form in New Orleans music, as preserved on records, is that the music is organized not about the "hot solo" alone, not the free ensemble alone, but by the interplay of melodic lines, a movement of the music through a constant series of "opposites," of instrumental contrasts. This may be called the "duet" or "concerto" principle. The latter term may seem inappropriate to many, thinking of the flamboyant and showy, classical concert-hall concerto, or of Gershwin's Concerto in F.

The concerto was born in European music and flourished, however, exactly out of such an interplay of solo instrument and massed tone as we have in jazz. This duet or concerto style of organization is basic to the music of King Oliver, of Morton, of Johnny Dodds' small groups, of the Louis Armstrong Hot Five and Hot Seven which collectively make up our best recorded heritage of New Orleans music. Solos in the later swing sense are rare, nor do all the instruments strike out on their own as proclaimed in the free improvisation theory. Rather there is the constant and conscious interplay of musical ideas. This interplay starts within the "cell" of the twelve or sixteen-bar theme itself, where we may have eight bars of "sweet" music answered by four bars of stop-time and breaks, a statement in harmonized melody, chromatic or in minor key, answered by a free blue ensemble; a half-chorus on a solo instrument answered by a half-chorus from another, a solo instrument answered by the full band.

King Oliver's records are of this kind, and full chorus solos are rarely found in them. Perhaps their greatest beauty is their use of breaks. Certainly the Oliver records have the finest collection of breaks, and of a music adorned by them, in the history of jazz; the musicians contributing them are Oliver himself, Louis Armstrong, Johnny Dodds and Honore Dutry. And these records exhibit the many varied forms of New Orleans jazz. "High Society" and "Tears" are in parade style, the latter in especially sweet style climaxed by a series of wonderful breaks, some of them by Armstrong and Oliver together. "Weatherbird," "Froggie Moore" and "Snake Rag" are in piano rag style; "Canal Street Blues" and "Chimes Blues" show a funeral, minor-key influence; "Dipper-mouth" is a wonderful example of the fast, stomp-style, twelve bar blues. "Jazzing Babies Blues" is a fine example of the use of the riff.

Ferdinand Morton's records show a similar variety, and are illuminated by wonderful duets and half-choruses, in which his own piano plays a prominent role, as well as the clarinet of Johnny Dodds, Omer Simeon and Albert Nicholas, the trumpet of Lee Collins, George Mitchell and Ward Pinkett, the trombone of Kid Ory and Geechy Fields, the banjo of Johnny St. Cyr, the drumming of Baby Dodds, and Tommy Benford. "Black Bottom Stomp" and "Steamboat Stomp" are in march style; "Wild Man Blues," "Beale Street Blues," "Jungle Blues" are beautiful examples of the half-chorus, duet style, and fine interplay of "hot" and "sweet" melodic lines. "The Pearls" and "The Chant" derive from the eccentric piano rag, and are adorned with beautiful breaks.

The Armstrong Hot Five and Hot Seven records use mainly a King Oliver personnel; Louis Armstrong, Johnny Dodds, Lillian Armstrong and Johnny St. Cyr, with Kid Ory instead of Dutry, on trombone, on the "Hot Five." Baby Dodds and a bass player, Pete Briggs or Ed Garland, are added for the "Hot Seven." "Skid-

Dat-De-Dat" is one of the most beautiful examples on record of a continual interplay of "hot" and "sweet" melodic lines, and is a most perfectly organized piece of music, the harmonized, minor-key, four-bar statement recurring throughout the entire piece, and answered by blues solo, blues "scat-singing" or blues ensemble. "Yes, I'm In the Barrel," "Gully Low Blues" and "Twelfth Street Rag" are fine examples of a rag and blues mixture, the last-named giving the familiar rag a fine, "slow drag," blues treatment. "Willie the Weeper" and "Muskat Ramble" are lusty marches. "Oriental Strut," "Potato Head Blues" and "Cornet Chop Suey" are examples of a sweet, sixteen-bar theme developed through a cumulative series of brilliant stop-time and break choruses. "Savoy Blues" is a fine example of music organized about the riff.

Another product of the rag-blues marriage was the kind of popular song which might be called New Orleans' gift to tin-pan-alley. These songs consisted, like the rags, of two sets of melodies, a sixteen-bar "verse" and a thirty-two bar "chorus." Some of these songs were almost straight twelve-bar blues, with an insertion of four bars of stop-time and break. Others were sweet in idiom, but with a hint of the blues break. Such songs make up a great body of the "blues" sung by Bessie Smith. Bessie Smith was not limited, of course, to any rigid type of song. She sang a wonderful twelve-bar blues, as in "Backwater Blues," "Money Blues," "Hard Drivin' Papa," "Lost Your Head Blues." With her magnificent voice

and personality she could even give a living character to
songs that show a tin-pan-alley silliness, especially in their
words, like "Muddy Water," "After You've Gone,"
"Alexander's Ragtime Band." But it was the sixteen-bar
rag blues, like "Young Woman's Blues," "One and Two
Blues," "I Ain't Goin' To Play Second Fiddle," "Lonesome Desert Blues," "Nobody Knows You When You're
Down and Out," that enabled her to build up her magnificent, fluid and dramatic song forms.

The ragtime songs produced by New Orleans composers had quality. Even in them, however, compared to
the folk blues, there begins a deterioration of the words.
Printed as sheet music, they were subject to a censorship
no less powerful because it was unwritten. This censorship was not one that eliminated dealing with sex. On
the contrary, true to the commercial mentality, it empha-
sized such themes, transforming them, however, from
an honest projection of realities of life into a double-
meaning lasciviousness. Other themes, depicting life as
it is actually lived among the poor and exploited, were
banned. As in Hollywood, this trade censorship "cleaned
up" the art into something dirtier and more hypocritical.

The growing insipidity of the words of these songs,
as well as the music, as they become an industrial product, tells us who is really responsible for the idiocy of our
misnamed "popular art." It proves that when the people
really produce art without interference, it has quality.
Bogus "popular art" is a reflection of the commercial

and publicity mentality. Bessie Smith sings these beautiful and touching words, in "Backwater Blues,"

> When it thunders and lightnings and the wind begins
>   to blow,
> And thousands of people ain't got no place to go. . . .
> I went and stood up on a high, old, lonesome hill,
> And looked down at the house where I used to live.

In "Muddy Water," however, we hear this nonsense,

> Dixie Moonlight, Swanee shore,
> Trees are whispering, come on back to me
> Muddy Water, hear my plea. . . .

"Jelly-Roll" Morton paints a realistic picture in "Mamie's Blues,"

> She stood on the corner, her feet just soaking wet,
> Beggin' each and every man that she met
> If you can't give a dollar, give me a lousy dime. . . .

Tin-pan-alley invents,

> If I could be with you one hour tonight,
> If I were free to do the things I might. . . .

Charles Edward Smith, describing Morton's "Don't You Leave Me Here," says, "the tonk world was a world of uncertain tomorrows, in which everyone was on his way somewhere. Figuratively speaking it was Alabama, and a popular saying had it: 'In places you are going you was supposed to be bound for that place.' Jelly-Roll told me of this, and added: 'So in fact I was Alabama bound'." We need only compare this image to the moronic commercial "Mammy" and "Alabammy Bound" songs to see what power is brought to art by the honesty to see and describe life as people live it, what havoc is wrought by the money mind when it imposes the content of its own conception of life.

New Orleans music was a national music of the Negro people, circumscribed by their impoverished ghetto life in the Southern city. New Orleans became a center for this music, because of its long musical traditions, having been, for more than a century, the most musical city of the South; the slightly freer social life enjoyed by the Negro people in this city; and its situation as a meeting place for folk music of many lands and cultures, combining the deep South, the far West, the Gulf Coast and Caribbean.

It provided the greatest opportunities for improvisation precisely because it possessed the most powerful musical forms, through which music became a social possession. It is through its unity of contrasting elements that we must understand this music; its interplay of "hot" and "sweet," of the deep blues and the many non-blue, musical languages; its free, sinuous melodic lines, full of freshness and surprise, along with familiar well-loved melodies, played affectionately and "straight"; its blazing breaks and quotable riffs; its single line of melody and its many-voiced ensembles; its strange dissonances and its simple harmonies; its economy of note and line; and its brilliant, intricate figuration. It even brought together Negro and white, on a beginning level, for although such collaboration could not take place openly, it was a music largely created by the Negro people that the white, Dixieland players consciously arranged and popularized. It was a good school for musicians, because music, within the narrow limits that the Negro could possess it, was a way of living as well as a way of making a living. Because it was so richly varied a music, in it may be found all the seeds of later jazz. Because it provided so great an opportunity for the individual musician to grow, it brought forth individual musicians of outstanding powers, who began to seek musical opportunities not permitted them in the exploited and jim-crowed life of the Negro in a Southern city.

Modern jazz is much different from New Orleans. It has to be. Yet we find its germs in New Orleans music. The blues have always been a vital part of jazz, as they are now. The basic beat of New Orleans blues and stomp jazz, the 4/4 beat, is still the basic beat of jazz. The various intensifications of beat that came later can be found hinted at in New Orleans music. We can find the "jump," beat, the two strongly accented and delayed off-beats to the bar, dominating the melodic line, in such works as Morton's "Beale St. Blues," Armstrong's and Ory's "Savoy Blues" and "Twelfth Street Rag." This beat became predominant in later Kansas City and large swing band jazz. The double jump, or "eight-to-the-bar" beat, may be found in the hop-scop blues, the walking bass, and several other New Orleans dance patterns. Even the rapid sixteenth note solo, familiar in bebop, may be found in the New Orleans clarinet solo. Forms based on the riff, so important in later large band jazz, may be found in New Orleans music. The play with chromatic figures, the series of dizzy modulations to distant keys and return home, a feature of the most modern jazz, may be found touched upon in New Orleans jazz. An amazing example is Omer Simeon's solo in the Morton trio record, "Shreveport."

New Orleans music brought forth a phenomenal group of creative musicians, like Joplin, Morton, Oliver and Armstrong, but it was only outside of New Orleans and the South that they were able to work out and expand the musical powers they had within them. Yet of them, it is possible to say that what they created was only a fraction of the music they could have brought into being. Already in New Orleans music the Negro people were proving that they had the power to give America its great composers, a great music on the highest levels. Our admiration for the creative genius of the outstanding Negro musicians must be tempered with a sense of loss as well; that, phenomenal as their music is, an even greater music was lost to us because of the narrow limitations forced upon them and the few materials with which they had to work. We must remember that, although the Negro people did not spend their time lamenting, but managed to wrest some joy out of their ghetto life, it was a horrible life.

W. C. Handy's autobiography, "Father of the Blues," for example, is not written in an uncheerful mood. Yet we can find some gruesome stories in it, such as the lynching of Louis Wright, a member of his group, while touring Missouri, or the time his entire group almost died of small-pox, denied even medicine or medical care, by the callous and selfish white people about them; or the games of fun-loving Texans who riddled their car with bullets as it sped through a town. We must remember that while the power of New Orleans music is a testament to the creative genius of the people who brought it into being, it was a circumscribed music. If we understand this, we can understand why the Negro jazz musician felt the need, and in fact demanded the right, to perfect his technique, to learn all there was to know about music, to study all the idioms, practises, forms and methods available to the rest of the American people.

Jazz had to break out of its New Orleans limitations. The closing down of the Storyville section of New Orleans in 1917, sometimes given in histories as the "turning point," was only one episode, and not too significant, in a much broader historical movement. The Negro people were demanding, and finding, means to travel, to move more freely, to enter into new jobs, to use their talents in ways denied to them by a jim-crowed life. The movement of jazz musicians North was one aspect of this heightened consciousness of rights which they were denied and opportunities that beckoned for a new maturity.

In breaking out of New Orleans, jazz became a possession of all America; Negro and white, North and South, Eastern seaboard and Pacific coast. It encountered many new problems of idiom, form and style, and of the relation of the jazz musician to American life. Its handling of these problems makes up the story of modern jazz. Its progress is far from over, and its problems far from solution. But its essential character has not changed. It is, today, the free, experimental and unregimented wing of American song and dance music, the battle-ground on which the musician fights for his independence, his right to create as a thinking and sensitive human being. It carries on now, as before, a constant struggle against standardization, limitation, jim-crow, the windy proclamations of advertisers and publicity, the unchecked hatred of commercial hacks who resent its independent life even as they take over its material.

Its continued life against constant odds points to the day when American popular music, as a whole, will be the honest music, the combination of the familiar and strange, the old and the new, the remembered myth and the fresh human experience, the well-loved language and the new, exciting variation, that will deserve the title of a people's music. It points to the day when music will again be both a social possession and an individual creation, but without the squalor, the poverty, the destruction of precious human material, that life among the Negro people was condemned to in the South and New Orleans.

RECORD ILLUSTRATIONS—CHAPTER FOUR

Blues Piano

JIM YANCEY
> Boogie Woogie Piano (in Victor Album P-25); Eternal Blues, How Long How Long Blues (Session 12001,3); Boodling (Session 10001); Bear Trap Blues (Columbia 37336)

MEADE LUX LEWIS
> Honky Tonk Train (Decca 18110, Columbia 37336); Chicago Flyer (Blue Note 39); Blues, Part 2 (From Blues, Part 1-4 Blue Note 8)

PETE JOHNSON
Kaycee on My Mind, Blues on the Down Beat (Decca 27264);
You Don't Know My Mind, Holler Stomp (Blue Note 12);
Roll 'em Pete (with Joe Turner) (Columbia 35959)

ALBERT AMMONS
Boogie Woogie Stomp, Boogie Woogie Blues (Blue Note 2);
Albert's Special Boogie, The Boogie Rocks (Commodore 617)

PINE TOP SMITH
Pinetop's Boogie Woogie, Pinetop's Blues, Jump Steady Blues,
I'm Sober Now (Brunswick Album B-1002)

"CRIPPLE" CLARENCE LOFTON
Early Blues, In The Morning, The Fives, South End Boogie
(Session 10006,2)

MONTANA TAYLOR
Barrelhouse Blues (Circle Album S-2)

Rag Piano

WALTER ROSE (with members of Lu Watter's Band)
Harlem Rag (West Coast 107)

FERDINAND MORTON
Original Rags, The Crave, The Naked Dance (Commodore
4001,2,3); Seattle Hunch (Victor 27565)

JAMES P. JOHNSON
Mule Walk Stomp, Caprice Rag (Blue Note 27, 26)

THOMAS "FATS" WALLER
Carolina Shout (Victor 27563)

EARL HINES
57 Varieties (Columbia 35875); Weatherbird (with Armstrong) (Columbia 36375)

BLIND LEROY GARNET
Louisiana Glide (Century 3025)

JOE SULLIVAN
Fidgety Feet (Disc 6003)

BABY DODDS TRIO
Wolverine Blues (Circle 1001)

New Orleans and "Dixieland" Instrumental Classics

High Society—RENA (Circle Album S-10); BECHET (Blue Note 50); ORY (Decca 25134); JOHNSON (Victor 40-0126)

Clarinet Marmalade—RENA (Circle S-10); BRUNIES (Commodore 549); BEIDERBECKE (Columbia 37804)

Jazz Me Blues—BECHET (Blue Note 44), HARTMAN (Keynote 601); BEIDERBECKE (Columbia 36156)

Muskat Ramble—BRUNIES (Commodore 618); ARMSTRONG (Columbia 36153); ORY (Decca 25133)

Diga Diga Doo—HARTMAN (Keynote 602); STEWART (HRS 2004)

At the Jazz Band Ball—BEIDERBECKE (Columbia 36156); DAVISON (Commodore 575)

Bailing the Jack (The World's Jazz Crazy); ORY (37277) DE PARIS (Blue Note 41)

Tin Roof Blues—HARTMAN (Keynote 601), BRUNIES (Commodore 556)

Weary Blues—RENA (Circle S-10); DODDS (Brunswick 80073)

Panama—RENA (Circle S-10); SULLIVAN-BECHET (Disc 6004); BRUNIES (Commodore 1511)

Eccentric—KAMINSKY (Commodore 560)

She's Crying for Me—HODES (Blue Note 506); WYNN (Brunswick 80042)

Twelfth Street Rag—ARMSTRONG (Columbia 35663)

Fidgety Feet, Sensation, Farewell Blues—EVANS (Disc 6071,2,5)

Milneburg Joys—RENA (Circle S-10)

Sugarfoot Stomp (with Oliver's "Dippermouth" solo); HODES (Blue Note 34)

Tiger Rag—ORY (Columbia 37274)

Ory's Creole Trombone—ARMSTRONG (Columbia 37634)

Creole Belles, Chattanooga Stomp—WATTERS (West Coast 102)

Songs Born of the Blues and Rags

BESSIE SMITH

Nobody Knows You When You're Down and Out (Columbia 37577); You've Been a Good Old Wagon, Cold in Hand (Columbia 35672); Young Woman's Blues (Columbia 35673)

KID ORY

Farewell to Storyville (Columbia 37277)

MUGGSY SPANIER
Sister Kate (Victor 40-0139); Memphis Blues (Commodore 1519)

ART HODES
Yellow Dog Blues (Blue Note 505)

EDDIE CONDON with JACK TEAGARDEN
Aunt Hagars Blues (Decca 24220)

LOUIS ARMSTRONG
West End Blues (Columbia 36377)

SIDNEY DE PARIS
Everybody Loves My Baby (Blue Note 40)

WILD BILL DAVISON
Baby Won't You Please Come Home (Commodore 575)

MIFF MOLE, with FRANK TESCHEMACHER
Shim-me-sha-wobble (Columbia 35953)

BUNK JOHNSON
Sister Kate (Victor 40-0128)

MILDRED BAILEY
Squeeze Me (Decca 18109)

ART HODES
Squeeze Me (Blue Note 35)

The line of demarcation between what I have called New Orleans classics, "Dixieland" music, and Songs born of Rags and Blues, is a very shadowy one. What we actually have here are three stages in the development of a music; first the traditional New Orleans dances and marches, the same general tune often given many different names; then the transformation and fixing of much of this music into set pieces such as Muskat Ramble, Clarinet Marmalade, High Society, Eccentric; then the ap-

pearance of published songs, like "Baby Won't You Please Come Home," "Yellow Dog Blues," "Sister Kate," which still talk the traditional language. These three stages overlap, and in following them on records, it is important to judge by ear rather than by the name. "Diga Diga Doo" and "Jazz Me Blues," while published as songs, make perfect instrumental rag material. "Clarinet Marmalade," generally played as a fast rag, is given a fine, folkish march treatment by the Rena band. While many of the justly renowned jazz performers take part in the recordings listed above, it is pleasant to notice what fine performances are turned in by many whose names would hardly have been known to collectors ten years ago, such as Centobie, Hartman, Laine, Robinson, Nicholas, Parenti, Carey, Darensbourg, and whose talents were uncovered with the growing attention to the folk and popular roots of jazz.

A great body of the most beautiful traditional and folk jazz is out of print, and should be restored to circulation. The most important is the series of records made by King Oliver's Creole Band, for Gennett and Okeh. Most of the Original Dixieland Jazz Band and New Orleans Rhythm Kings compositions are available today on much better-sounding records than the originals, but the old versions are still worth knowing. The list of Johnny Dodds and Ferdinand "Jelly-Roll" Morton records reissued by Victor on its Bluebird label during the 'thirties, including more than thirty sides of extraordinary inter-

est and beauty, like Dodds' "Weary City," "Bucktown Stomp," "Bull Fiddle Blues," "Indigo Stomp," "Goober Dance," and Morton's "The Chant," "Jungle Blues," "Wild Man Blues," "Black Bottom Stomp," "Beale St. Blues," "Steamboat Stomp," "Doctor Jazz," "Blue Blood Blues," "Shreveport," demands restoration. Some great Armstrong Hot Five sides are still out of print, such as "Lonesome Blues" and "Willie the Weeper," and a great number of Bessie Smith's finest performances, such as "Second Fiddle," "St. Louis Blues," "Backwater Blues," "Hard Driving Papa," "Jazzbo Brown." A fresh series made by Sidney Bechet for Victor, during the 'thirties, with some fine players such as J. C. Higginbotham, Henry Allen, Sandy Williams, had much interesting traditional music, and is now unavailable, as is the Dixieland series made by Muggsy Spanier, with Cless and Brunies, for Bluebird.

The out-of-print-disease affects small companies as well as large ones, but for different reasons; the inability to keep up a necessarily hand-to-mouth existence, and the difficulty of competing with the large companies in distribution. Blues piano is well represented on available records, but a fine series recorded by Dan Qualey on Solo-Art, including Pete Johnson's "Pete's Blues," Jim Yancey's "The Fives," and extraordinary sides by Lewis, Ammons and others, has disappeared. The Session records are listed because of their great quality, and the fact that the company is still in operation, but the Yancey records have been lately unavailable. What American invention and industrialization gives us on the one hand, the market system takes away on the other.

The Morton records originally made under the supervision of Alan Lomax for the Library of Congress, and now issued by Circle, are in a special category; available, but only as a complete set of twelve albums of forty-five records. On them Morton tells of New Orleans life as he remembers it, and illustrates his anecdotes with some of the most beautiful piano jazz ever recorded. Without pretending to be the entire story of either the life or the music, it is the most important and authentic single document dealing with the roots and local color of jazz music.

CHAPTER FIVE

THE POP TUNE, THE HOT SOLO & THE LARGE BAND

No other city holds a place in jazz history comparable to that of New Orleans. The reason is that New Orleans jazz itself was more than the music of a city. It was the concentrated music of the entire lower Mississippi valley, Texas and the Gulf Coast. It was a people's music, predominantly created by the Negro people. After its movement out of New Orleans, jazz became a music of all America, loved and performed by all peoples; a music that could no longer be called characteristic of the life in a single city or locality, or characteristic solely of the Negro people.

Even in the New Orleans period, jazz had become a music of white people as well as Negro. A language of dance, poetry and song with such realistic, evocative power found a response in all who came in contact with it. Even those attached to hidebound ways of music were slowly changed in their musical thinking. The Negro people created such a language because they themselves were meeting the world on the sharpest, most harsh and demanding terms, as the laboring people in the front line of man's struggle against nature. Their art reflected this struggle; showed the lines it engraved in the human mind and body. It was an art of powerful, realistic human images and concentrated emotional strength.

And this culture entered the mind of the Southern white people, although many would be shocked at the thought of such an influence and debt. This influence had earlier taken place with the spirituals, which drew much of their material from prevalent hymns and mountain tunes, transformed it and gave back a new art to white people. The blues were even more widely influenced by the general body of American folk music, and in turn adopted by the white people.

The influence became overwhelming with jazz. The first jazz band to make a nation-wide success was the

Original Dixieland Jazz Band, made up of five white musicians. The music they played was their own invention, put together with fine taste. Yet it was a music wholly drawn in material from the Negro contributions. As jazz became increasingly popular, its idiom permeated the rising music industry; thousands of pieces of diluted New Orleans music in the form of blues, torch songs, rag-time songs, one-steps, two-steps and fox-trots were produced. Tin-pan-alley in the 1910's and '20's was open to genuinely new ideas, unlike the music factory it has become today, part of the Hollywood, radio and phonograph record network. Sons of immigrant families who had brought a love of music with them from Europe to New York eagerly amalgamated this tradition with the wealth of new forms and ideas brought by jazz. The stream of music thus produced had many weaknesses, but also real quality. The beloved American popular music of song and dance is a creation first of the Negro people, and then of Jewish, Irish, Italian and other "minority" peoples. It has become part of the consciousness even of snobs who would shudder at the idea of rubbing elbows with the people who gave them this music.

New Orleans music itself brought about conditions which forced it out of the confines of Southern life. A communal and collectively created music, it produced musicians of such developing powers that they themselves began to seek a home where they could expand their ideas, spread themselves in their music, learn the full art of music, handle all its resources, and get for themselves some of the decencies of life. Because the music had such great appeal to all people, it sought a place where the collaboration between Negro and white musicians, the exchange of ideas, could go on openly and unreservedly, instead of through the subterranean channels available to it in the South.

It was such a role that Chicago, New York and the other cities of the North played in the development of jazz. It was sometimes thought that Chicago had contributed an important new style to jazz, "Chicago Style" as opposed to "New Orleans" style. This theory disappeared with the realization that jazz is a music more than a "style," and Chicago jazz was mainly a refinement of New Orleans music. Yet Chicago and New York are important names in the history of jazz. In both a great Negro community lived under conditions of comparative freedom. The Negro community in the North was and is segregated; its housing conditions continue the most backward, and its rents the highest. Its people are forced into the lowest paid jobs and are the first to be unemployed. Yet their range of freedom was a good step beyond that of New Orleans, and the struggle for new stages was made possible.

The music reflected both the changed status of the musician and the changed temper of the audience. It showed in new technique, in more massive sound, in the handling of new harmonic materials, in more elaborate, individual contributions. The collaboration in music making between Negro and white musicians became more open, with an increasingly frank acknowledgement of the debt owed by the white American people to the Negro. A new jazz began to take shape.

These steps forward did not settle the problems of jazz. In Chicago, however, it may be said that the battle against jim-crow, and segregation, was taken up consciously and militantly by jazz musicians. It was a forward step for young white musicians in Chicago to listen with admiration to King Oliver, Louis Armstrong, Bessie Smith, Jimmy Noone, Fletcher Henderson's great aggregation of players; to be proud to sit on the stand with them; to adopt their music, and openly acknowledging their debt.

A new step was the making of records together, in which Eddie Condon pioneered. At first there was no public acknowledgement of the collaboration. What often happened was that the white musicians joined in the making of "race" records, as blues jazz recordings were chauvinistically known. With the rise of small hot jazz recording outfits, such as HRS and Commodore, the names of the players were listed and the collaboration was made public. It was a great further achievement when Benny Goodman added the Negro players, Teddy Wilson and Lionel Hampton to his band. The practise was taken up by Artie Shaw and Gene Krupa. But the fact that musical organizations should be made up of people whose ability is measured by their musicianship, not their skin color or ancestry, is still not accepted by radio stations, the moving picture industry, most band managements. The Negro musician is still the lowest paid—jimcrowed out of a vast number of jobs he has the abilities to fill. Meanwhile the music he invents and creates draws enormous money returns—mainly for others.

In this new environment a great deal of fresh and exciting music has been produced, along with an even greater amount of unsuccessful, or semi-successful work. It is far from having achieved its full goals. The intricate problems being tackled by jazz musicians today have to be mastered under adverse conditions. It is a herculean task to create as a thinking and creative musician working long, night-club hours in a liquor-laden atmosphere, suffering more unemployment than employment, doing one-night stands, getting poor pay, being under constant pressure from managers for quick novelties and from publicity agents for sensations. Mozart and Beethoven could not have done much under such conditions.

But music, like history, has a movement which can be checked but not turned backward. It was inevitable that in the change from a folk and a communal music to a highly individual music, qualities should be lost as well as gained. Silly theories have been spun out of the loss, with anguished outcries of "decadence," "degeneration," "European influences," "commercialization"; the latter term being loosely used to characterize not only the music truly commercial, but all jazz music using new musical materials. It is true that modern jazz is lacking in many memorable qualities of New Orleans music; but it is also true that modern jazz has made rich additions to our musical culture. It has provided a musical expression for feelings which could not be encompassed within New Orleans music. The life that produced New Orleans music was now a thing of the past; to repeat this music could only be an academic exercise, adding little to the music we already know. To keep this music alive, to keep performing it, is an important task, for it has too many great qualities to be forgotten. But such performances can be only one part of a living musical culture.

We can find an analogy in the development of nineteenth century music in Europe. Academic scholars complained that the "new" music of Berlioz, Schumann, Chopin, Lizst, Wagner and Mussorgsky was inferior in form to that of Bach, Handel and Mozart in the previous century. Our present day tastes may confirm this complaint. But attempts to recreate music in the old forms only resulted in the comparatively sweet symphonies and oratorios of Mendelssohn, and Saint-Saens, and much altogether poor music produced in great quantities and quickly forgotten. The new music had to take the path of Schumann, Berlioz and Wagner. And if this music proved to be one-sided, or insufficient to meet all of people's needs, the remedy lay in going still further forward, not backward; in studying the past, but only to re-create the social qualities of the past on a higher level, including the new discoveries in musical techniques and expression of human emotions. This is the great problem facing composed music today. It is also the problem being worked out in jazz.

Even the music we now know as New Orleans could only have been made known to us by the movement North. We study New Orleans music today largely from the records of Joe Oliver, Ferdinand Morton, Louis Armstrong of the Hot Five and Seven days, Bessie Smith, the Original Dixieland Jazz Band. These records were made in and around New York and Chicago. It may be said that this music is a New Orleans music, but a reservation is necessary.

The Negro community for whom Oliver played in Chicago was different from the Negro community in New Orleans. The music that Oliver played was still New Orleans in its march tempo, its rag, blues and stomp content, its collective music making and self-absorption in the music on the part of the players; but it also reflected the new Chicago audience. The opportunity to make records, as well, induced a greater attention to technical detail and formal organization, making the music a rounded out unity with beginning, middle and end.

In Bessie Smith's records there is, likewise, a new spirit expressed in old materials. Along with the rich folk qualities of her performances, there is a sense of conflict and freedom, an assertion of individual independence, a fine and subtle artistry and musical organization, which bespeaks a comparative freedom of movement and speech on the part of the musician.

The same is true of Morton's records, which show him to be a fine, individual artist and composer as well as a master of folk materials. His records are still an invaluable source of study of New Orleans music, for it is of New Orleans city life that they speak. They combine the "educated" piano rags and the deep blues, the marches and stomps, the breaks and riffs, the fine individual improvisations in solo and ensemble. He could make his composed pieces sound improvised. He was an arranger who carefully calculated the position of every break, the interweaving of harmonic, chordal passages with free improvisation, the interplay of sweet melodies with blues, the duets between one instrument, notably his own fine piano, and clarinet or guitar, in a performance that sounded like improvisation. The perfection of the best Morton records, like "Jungle Blues," "Black Bottom Stomp," "The Pearls," "The Chant," "Beale St. Blues," "Wild Man Blues," "Blue Blood Blues," the trio records, is never an accident; nor is it entirely typical except in its material, of the music customarily heard in New Orleans. It is a composed music.

The Armstrong Hot Five and Hot Seven records, made with Johnny Dodds, Edward Ory, Johnny St. Cyr, Lillian Armstrong, and, at times, Baby Dodds, Lonnie Johnson, Pete Briggs and Ed Garland, are New Orleans in style and material. It took a whole people to bring into being a music like "Willie the Weeper," "Savoy Blues," "Muskat Ramble," "Twelfth St. Rag," "Yes, I'm in the Barrel," "Potato Head Blues," "Skid-dat-de-dat," "Cornet Chop Suey," "Gully Low Blues," "Lonesome Blues," "King of the Zulus," with their rich evocations of march, of celebration, of bitter humor, of poignant lament and masked protest. But, within the general New Orleans style of perfect collaboration and interchange among the soloists, there is a great expansion of the solo voice. Armstrong and Dodds play solos of a magnitude and scope not found in the Oliver band performances. It is at once New Orleans music and a new creation.

Oliver, Morton, Bessie Smith, advanced on no easy road. Oliver died in poverty. Morton never fulfilled his great creative talents. Bessie Smith was sometimes penniless, and died of jim-crow. She was hurt in an automobile accident near Memphis, and the story has it that either through being refused admittance by one hospital after another, or being left to be treated late, she died from loss of blood.

Louis Armstrong achieved financial success, by using his phenomenal talent to meet, head on, the new conditions of musical life. These were the conditions generally described as commercialism. The term commercialism should not be applied, however, to the desire of the musician to be paid for his work, and paid commensurate with his talents. Neither should it be applied to the desire of the jazz musician to use the prevailing musical language of his period and audience. The step from the amateur or semi-amateur status of most of the New Orleans musicians, to the status of a musician paid for his work and making a profession of it, was a progressive step.

Commercialism should be restricted, as a term, to what is really destructive in culture; the taking over of an art, in this case popular music, by business, and the rise of business to so powerful a force in the making of music that there was no longer a free market for the musicians. Instead of distribution serving the musician, distribution, where the money was invested, became the dominating force, dictating both the form and content of the music. It tended to force the musician into the status of a hired craftsman whose work was not supposed to bear his own individuality, free thought and exploration of the art, but was to be made to order, to a standardized pattern.

The free market that existed when the industry was small had been a benefit to jazz, enabling musicians like W. C. Handy, Clarence Williams, Oliver, Armstrong, Morton and others to break out of the confines of New Orleans life. As the music industry became more monopolized, as radio, sound pictures, and the electric phonograph record made the music producing industry a center of large capital investment, the tendency was to avoid the interplay of artist and audience that makes for active entertainment and great art, and to substitute a pseudo-entertainment depending largely on shallow novelty offered to a passive, undemanding audience. Music was keyed down to the minimum that would be acceptable to everybody, and consequently had little meaning for anybody. Tune producers no longer depended on public approval. Tie-ups were made with singers, bands and song-pluggers, with radio and Hollywood, controlling songs before they were written, and song writers had to turn out the tunes according to specifications as if they were producing frankfurters. Radio and juke-box destroyed the economic base for the small band. The factory-produced popular tunes overwhelmed the blues, rags, and folk song germs with a harmonic idiom taken from nineteenth century concert music.

Armstrong's going over to the large band and the popular tune has been criticized by some whose predilection for New Orleans music blinds them to hard facts. The most extreme statement of the case is that made by Rudi Blesh, in "Shining Trumpets." He laments that Armstrong did not integrate his "genius" with the "music, and thus ultimately the destiny, of his race," thereby failing in his task of filling "the overwhelming and immemorial need of his own race to find a Moses to lead it out of Egypt." Such statements betray ignorance.

First, "race" itself is an unscientific and meaningless term. The Negro people of America, in ancestry and physiology, are not a race. There is no special and limited

"music" of the Negro people. They have a right to know
and use all music, making it their own, as they took over
whatever music they needed in the past. The Negro people are not waiting for a "Moses" to lead them out of
"Egypt." They are putting up a collective struggle, for
the right to live as free human beings on equal terms
with anybody else. Lastly, the causes of discrimination
and the special exploitation Negroes suffer, are not such
as could have been changed by Armstrong playing New
Orleans music instead of popular songs with large bands.
Certainly his early records are among the most beautiful
pieces of music-making in which he ever took part. But
had he continued playing "Dippermouth" and "Gully
Low" for the rest of his life, with small combinations, it
is hard to see how this would have abolished jim-crow,
segregation, lynching, or the poll-tax. The end of such a
course would probably have been starvation.

Those New Orleans musicians such as Sidney Bechet
and Johnny Dodds, who continued to perform small
band blues, produced a great deal of beautiful music,
although this music did not appreciably change the status
of the Negro people in America. It is also true that there
are some aspects of Armstrong's career which one may
regret. Occasionally he had to succumb to the pressure
exerted upon every member of a minority group, Negro,
Jewish, Italian or any other, who rises in the entertainment world, to clown and to mock his own people. This
savage form of prejudice, disguised as humor, is none the

less powerful because it is never openly expressed. It becomes a matter of unwritten law that the "straight" role in any production be played by someone disguised as an Anglo-Saxon stereotype, while the "comic" is reserved for a member of the minority group. Nor does this comedy have any relation to the great traditions of joyousness and satire in comedy. Some of Armstrong's records, such as "You Rascal You," "Shine" and "When It's Sleepy Time Down South" would not be made today, when our resentment of such insults directed against the peoples who together made America, is much sharper.

Armstrong's career is not one of great and unbroken growth. But progress in musical, as in social life, is made by coping with realities, not ignoring them. He made the best he could out of the conditions he found in the new entertainment world. He played with large bands such as Fletcher Henderson's, and then organized his own. He performed the general run of sweetened blues and popular songs. A master virtuoso on his instrument, a restless mind in search of new musical ideas, a creative musician always seeking to make music a fresh and personal experience, he stood this material on its head.

It was inevitable that the style should change, and the point of concentration should fall upon the solo instrument and the solo chorus. It may seem to be a contradiction, but it is almost inevitable that, as more instruments are added to a group, the music must become increasingly individual; based either on the solo instrument

and solo chorus, or, as in the case of bands such as Ellington's, on the arranger and composer. We can see this
change take place even in the small-band records that
Armstrong made after he had been playing with large
bands. Records such as "Basin St. Blues," "West End
Blues," "Tight Like This," "Knocking a Jug," are no
longer an ensemble music, although Earl Hines plays on
the first three and an array of fine performers, including
Jack Teagarden, play on the fourth. Sweet chords are
very much in evidence, although the material is still basically the blues. The greatness of these records lies in the
series of Armstrong choruses that end them. These are
magnificent integrated and climactic musical constructions, the trumpet piling phrase upon phrase, adorning
its melodic line with its own broken chords, rising to a
compelling climax and resolution. A new kind of jazz
emerges, and a new Armstrong, who can be called, even
though he still improvises, a full-fledged composer of
music.

It is at this point that we can say that things might
have been different and better. Had a genuine, musical
culture existed in America, one capable of cherishing its
talents and giving them a chance to properly learn and
grow, instead of destroying them, Armstrong might have
been encouraged to produce a great American music.
There was no such opportunity, however; instead, the
continual pressure to produce novelties, to plug new
songs, or the same songs under new names. That Arm-

strong had the powers to produce a much greater music than he actually did is true. This however is different from saying that the musical "genius" of a people requires them to be limited to a folk culture and folk status; a culture, furthermore, that the conditions of life themselves had done away with.

As a sign of the change brought by the new form, the records of this period that attempt to preserve the old collective methods are comparatively weaker. A form in which one performer after another takes a solo chorus is weak to start with. Records like "Save it Pretty Mama," "Squeeze Me," "No One Else But You," are poor in all-over impact, although Armstrong's solos are little gems, and Hines does most inventive and pleasing work.

The great problem of the new jazz was a new musical form; a replacement for the form of New Orleans music which had been the creation of the community. Now the creation of form came from the individual. Armstrong, fronting a large band, recorded some magnificent pieces of single-handed musical construction. "Mahogany Hall Stomp" and "St. Louis Blues" (in the first versions made for Okeh), are such works. In both he builds up a stunning series of choruses, made up of riff figures within the harmonies set by the band, changing the riff with each chorus, simplifying it down to a single, long-drawn note and then expanding it into two and three note figures. Armstrong also created a kind of three-part form to deal with the popular tune. He begins with a solo chorus in which he plays close to the tune, but with a hot intonation and delayed attack that begins to give the tune a greater distinction than its composer had dreamed of. Then he sings a chorus, in which the song is kidded in both words and music, satirized and shown up for the nonsense it generally is. Last, the tune is transformed completely into a lyrical trumpet improvisation. The most famous example is "I Can't Give You Anything But Love." Other fine examples are "Stardust," "The Peanut Vendor," "Wrap Your Troubles in Dreams," "That's My Home," "On the Sunny Side of the Street." Then there are some records in which Louis gives his trumpet virtuosity and sense of humor a wild ride, as "Tiger Rag" and "Dinah," throwing in snatches of blues, other popular tunes, marches and opera; such performances hint at the coming bebop.

Such performances are no "decadence" but a genuine musical triumph, an addition to permanent American musical literature. Yet they rise as music out of a fierce struggle, between the performer and his material, a struggle to give the material a distinction it lacks in the original. This is the opposite situation to that of New Orleans music, where the material lent itself so easily to improvisation and musical construction. The struggle shows itself in the music. Even at its best, it is not relaxed, as the best of New Orleans is. The strain on the performer is a heavy one, precisely because he is working against his material. When to this strain is added the constant drive for novelty, made necessary by the position of a successful entertainer in the big-time musical world; the lack of time for the serious musical thinking which this new material and its problems require; the insecurity of a bandsman's career, and the unwholesome conditions surrounding the jazz performer's life; the night clubs, long hours, liquor and narcotics that became occupational diseases of jazz; the demands of agents and managers for repetition of successful mannerisms; it is obvious that the strain must soon become overpowering.

Armstrong was always, as he is today, a master of the instrument. There is hardly an Armstrong performance without some touch of musical distinction and interest. But solos inevitably begin to sound much like previous ones, the tunes they are based on being in themselves so poor and uninspiring. The performer begins to lead a double musical life, and it is especially the least creative that is put on records. Armstrong might have become a much greater musician than he now is. The fault however lies with the entertainment world in which he had to operate, one in which there was no living response between the artist and his audience, little real entertainment, little chance to grow.

Entertainment is a word with many meanings. In its truest sense, it means great art. The greatest art is the most entertaining. It gives an audience the unforgettable excitement of unfolding a new idea and experience, a fresh revelation of a human personality. Such entertainment is possible, however, only when an audience, itself, knows something of creation, or is willing to use its mind, to think, to enter into active collaboration with the artist. Commercially created entertainment, in its monopoly stage, is something quite different. It is the product of a factory system which saps the people of their creative powers, deprives them of their opportunity to produce a cultural life of their own. It offers them a "bought" entertainment, which they are to absorb passively. That this entertainment is never entertaining is seen in the frantic search of its producers, radio, moving picture or music publishing, for "novelty," combined with a fear and hatred of the true novelty of honest art production. Fresh creative figures who makes their way into this entertainment world are not encouraged to grow, but rather to be "typed," to repeat themselves. Such demands make growth itself a struggle against overwhelming obstacles.

Armstrong's music represents not a passive acceptance of this world of superficial entertainment, but a struggle against the conditions it imposed, an attack upon its material. He did not consciously plan his music as such an attack, but being a musician of taste and independence, he transformed everything he played. He did not take over a ready-made commercial style, but created a new style of performing popular tunes. His kidding vocals became taken up by many other singers, some of them not knowing why they were doing what they did, but only feeling that the audience responded better to a less cloying sentiment. He explored the full powers of the trumpet, so that players like Henry Allen, Roy Eldridge, Joe Guy, John Gillespie, Howard McGhee may be said to have walked in his tracks, technically.

He built up a new kind of solo, using the popular tune as a bass line and creating a new counter melody, bolstered by broken chords. This style had a powerful effect not only upon trumpet performance but upon other instruments as well. Higginbotham adapted similar ideas to the trombone, Hines to the piano. It is wrong to speak glibly of direct "influences," since it is possible for different musicians to work out the same ideas independently. But Armstrong's solo work parallels much of modern saxophone solo style. His chords did not move into the harmonic extremes of bebop, but the method he used was basic to bebop and modern jazz. His work underlined and carried to a high level of solution the major new problem that faced the creative jazz musician from the late twenties onward; that of making good music out of the popular ballad and diatonic, major-minor harmonic system.

Many other jazzmen of great talent coped with this problem; Thomas "Fats" Waller, James P. Johnson, Frank Newton, Earl Hines, Jimmie Noone; all of them men with a complete grounding in blues and rag music, and with great technical and inventive powers. Waller was the most prolific recorder among them and the consistently high level of his work is remarkable. As a pianist he was not as brilliant in his suspended rhythms and right hand figurations as Hines. I doubt whether any of his solo piano performances will live as the best of Hines' will. He had a powerful, left hand however, capable of providing, in itself, the full rhythm needed by a small band. With an engaging melodic invention as well, he managed to give all of his performances a richly personal flavor. As Armstrong did, but even more boisterously, he kidded the songs that came his way, and made up his own witty pieces of word and music. And, although his records have many fine solos and instrumental spots contributed by his band members, his personality dominates. The material he works with being what it is, the personality has to rise in spite of and in struggle against it. The result is that, while the Waller records are a joy to hear, and the music-making is on a consistently high level, it is hard to choose some above others, or select any that are really impressive and lasting contributions to American music, as the finest of jazz is. The best that can be said is that they entertain without insult to the intelligence, and loom up high above the common run of commercial musical tripe.

A great mass of hot jazz falls into a narrow, light-entertainment category, making an authoritative selection of better or lasting works almost impossible. The line between good music and bad becomes difficult to trace. The commercial music begins to take on qualities of hot jazz, and even includes performers of great talent. The hot music begins to take on something of the character of the commercial, due to the conditions under which it has to work, the language it must use, the weak forms and passive audiences. A great mass of jazz music is partly good, partly bad. Cliches which sound hot are mixed with passages of genuine hot invention. And this situation is found not only in the large "swing" bands but in the new small groups that take shape for recording or night-club performances.

This situation was not wholly bad. If hot jazz was apparently merging with much of what was loosely termed "commercial," the level of commercial music was immeasurably raised. Due to the irrepressible efforts of jazz players, most of them Negro, they made a creative music out of popular song idiom, the great American public was hearing a music more interesting and distinctive in instrumental texture, cleaner in melodic profile; a music of stimulation and surprises that began to teach audiences how to listen to music. And some of the groups that played it, both large bands like Lunceford's and Berigan's, and small groups like those formed about Teddy Wilson, Benny Goodman, Billie Holiday, Art Tatum, John Kirby, "Red" Norvo, Lionel Hampton, were a kind of experimental laboratory of the new hot jazz. The results of this experimentation may be seen in the jazz taking shape today.

Roughly parallel to the time when Armstrong was wrestling with the solo style and the popular tune, the same problem was being tackled by Leon "Bix" Beiderbecke. Bix did not get his trumpet or cornet style out of thin air. He studied Oliver, Armstrong, Joe Smith, Bessie Smith, Nick La Rocca of the Original Dixieland Five and Paul Mares of the New Orleans Rhythm Kings, both from records and in live performances. But his solo choruses on popular songs are most individual and personal creations. His solution, like that of Armstrong, shows that the next step for creative jazz, because of the conditions under which it now operated, had to be the greater emergence of the individual.

This is not to say that Bix was an individualist. Nobody in jazz history had more of a belief than he in collective and group creation. In fact, listening to the small-band Dixieland or semi-Dixieland records he made, we may regret the fact that Bix was so self-effacing. There is more Bix music on records than is actually played by him, and it is generally his music that we are hearing in the melodic figurations and breaks of a Miff Mole, Bill Rank, Don Murray, Frankie Trumbauer, Lennie Hayton and others who played with him. Bix played one of the most perfect, stimulating, Dixieland style, melodic leads. Even in his performances on popular songs, Bix will often end a record with a drive to give the entire ensemble a lift, as in "Sorry," "Singing the Blues," "Thou Swell," "Royal Garden Blues," "Louisiana," "Old Man River." It is only with such large groups as Paul Whiteman's that influencing the entire performance becomes impossible, and Bix handles only his own solo chorus or half chorus.

The individual sound of Bix's music has given rise to arguments as to whether he played "real" jazz. Such discussions must always be fruitless, because they attempt to cut a living art down to a mechanical formula. What formula can define "real" jazz? If jazz is "pure blues," then the music that Bunk Johnson and Kid Rena play on their records is often not "real jazz." If jazz is to adhere strictly to what Bunk Johnson, Kid Rena and Joe Oliver do, then the later Armstrong, Lester Young, Ellington are not jazz performers. But theirs is a music that grew out of jazz, and resembles exactly no other music heard or written. Jazz can be defined, but only in terms of a flexible, growing art, which changes as the conditions under which it is performed change, and because thinking individuals arise who, responding to new needs, add something new to something old. The "something new" is to be judged not by whether it is simply new or old, but by whether it is a genuine addition to the music, an addition to its human content, technique and expressive breadth. When it is such an addition, it is "real jazz," precisely because it is different, and because experiment and change are in the essence of jazz.

Beiderbecke, as an individual creative mind, has about the same relationship to the Original Dixieland Five music, out of which he grew, as Armstrong has to New Orleans music and Teschemacher to the Chicago version of Dixieland. And he stands for a most important historical step in jazz; the emergence of a creative, white man's jazz. This is not to say that jazz was thereby improved, or in any respect "taken away" from the Negro people. It is rather a testimony to the power of jazz music, and the great debt that Americans of all national origins owe to their Negro fellow citizens. Music is both a universal and national language. It takes on many national differences, which in turn develop and grow by learning from one another. And so it is one of the great achievements of jazz that it gave so many people, other than the Negro musicians, a chance to develop as musical creators. From Chicago days onward, the Negro musicians have learned a great deal from white musicians, as they have learned by beginning to assimilate the world body of composed music. The main influence, of course, is still in the other direction. The leaders in jazz progress have been mainly the Negro musicians, and the white musicians have learned far more than they have taught. Yet this give and take is a healthy approach to the national musical question in America; an approach that has yet to be made in other aspects of our lives.

Bix was hampered as a jazz musician, as many of the Chicago players were, by not knowing the blues as a living, flexible language. What he knew of the blues was generally taken from records, and some live performances. Thus many effects in his music, like those in later Chicago performances, the jumpy rhythmic pattern and off-beat flare-ups, are mannerisms, their reason for being not seen in the music itself. And yet his place is in the continuity of jazz and the blues. The rhythmic patterns of his solos are those of rag music, with their delayed attack, off-beat accents, slow phrases and sustained notes against a fast-moving beat. His breaks are beautiful and blue, concentrated sometimes down to a single "surprise" note, taking off from the preceding chord. He uses the blue note, although the off-pitch feeling is achieved almost imperceptibly, by delicate tonal shading. His solos derive from the blues style, often hitting an interval of a fourth when the ear expects a third, delighting the ear with its strangeness and rightness, accenting the surprise note as if to hint at a temporary transition to a distant key.

His language is not of the deep blues, as the Negro people of the South sang them. He brought to jazz music a partly fresh language of his own. "Davenport Blues" (his record of which is not particularly good), is an example of his melodic invention; a tender lyricism just skirting the edge of sentimentality. One misses the anger, bitterness, lament and proclamation of independence of the basic blues, but his feeling is still genuine, very much like the mid-West folk song that may also be heard in jazz through some of the Kansas City and Ellington blues.

Bix made many records but is not well represented on them. We get an idea of his powers by piecing sections of them together, and imagining the music multiplied. But there is still much fine music on them. His performances of Dixieland compositions, such as "Clarinet Marmalade" and "At the Jazz Band Ball" are among the most beautiful in existence, although the tailgate trombone is absent, as is a first-class clarinet line. His solos on popular tunes are almost wholly on the "chorus," as in the new manner. The live verse-chorus relationship, a product of the rags which gave New Orleans music so many interesting structural possibilities, has disappeared, as it disappeared in the tin-pan-alley songs originally inspired by rags. But these solos are beautiful pieces of original, creative music, tearing up the old melody to create out of its fragments a music of infinitely greater distinction. These solos, like those on "Way Down Yonder in New Orleans," "I'm Coming Virginia," "Singing the Blues," "Crying all Day," are full of strange touches and mix tender with strong, soft with staccato timbres. They are compact and rounded-out musical designs.

Bix's piano writing is a further stage of his development, outlining another path that has become important to jazz. Handling the popular tunes meant handling the diatonic major-minor chords and key relationships implicit in them. These could not be ignored, and so, to give his music freshness, the musician began playing about with the chords themselves, expending them into sevenths and ninths, adding chromatic notes, raising or lowering the tones of traditional "sweet" chords, with the eventual result that the popular tunes themselves vanished from the scene, the musician creating an original music out of their harmonic idiom. The blues re-enter, although greatly transformed. This is the character of "In a Mist" and some of the other Bix piano fragments. It hints at the piano playing of Theolonius Monk, Errol Garner, and in fact much of bebop.

A charge frequently made about this music is that it derives from Debussy, or other "European borrowings." Similar charges have been aimed at Ellington. This is another example of narrow and illogical thinking. The easiest kind of criticism is to find resemblances and transform them into "influences." Actually there are plenty of "Europeanisms" even in New Orleans music. There is no musical purity. If some hot jazz seems to resemble Debussy, it is because jazzmen were dealing with the same musical problems with which Debussy was dealing, and arrived at similar conclusions. Debussy, breaking away from strict diatonic music, trying to introduce exotic and folk scales into his textures, evolved fresh harmonic practises and fresh uses of instrumental timbre. If jazz, in its own development and its own language, begins to parallel the musical invention of a genius like Debussy, that is a great compliment to jazz and testimony to its musical vitality. The music, for all its real or fancied resemblance, is based on a language that is unique to jazz.

Bix was another example of a musician who may have had the genius to become a fine composer. He died of the occupational disease of the jazz entertainment world, the unsettled life, unhealthy hours, almost irrepressible need for stimulants; stimulants used not for musical needs, as some loose thinking puts it, but to make up temporarily for other lacks in a jazz performer's life. Stimulants, when they actually affect the music, always hurt it. Bix's music, however fragmentary, outlines as Armstrong does in a fuller way many of the problems raised by jazz from its Chicago days to the present.

The new music created by Louis and then Bix gives us a perspective from which to view the achievements and limitations of the "Chicago Style" musicians. A group of young players, gathering about the nucleus of the "Austin High School Boys," they studied the great jazz being played in Chicago by the New Orleans bands and worked out, collectively, a jazz of their own based on these models. This "Chicago" jazz is not, as was once thought, in any way comparable to New Orleans, for it did not produce a new music of its own. It was, however, an important step forward in jazz. It produced some remarkable and sensitive craftsmen of jazz, who made almost an analytic science of their art; the trumpet of Jimmy McPartland, Bobby Hackett, Max Kaminsky, "Wild" Bill Davison and Billy Butterfield, the clarinet of Rod Cless, "Mezz" Mezzrow, and Benny Goodman; the piano of Joe Sullivan and Jess Stacy; the drums of Dave Tough and George Wettling; the valve trombone of Brad Gowans, the guitar of Eddie Condon and Carmen Mastren, the tenor sax of Bud Freeman, the string bass of Jim Lannigan, Artie Shapiro, and Artie Bernstein. Although it tended towards a precise, "on the beat" and harmonically sweet jazz, it also produced some who offered a "gutty," rough-timbred, succinct and deeply felt jazz based on a genuine feeling for blues line and timbre; the trumpet of Francis "Muggsy" Spanier, the clarinet of Frank Teschemacher and "Pee Wee" Russell, the trombone of Floyd O'Brien, the piano of Art Hodes.

We have to look at this "Chicago" jazz not as one thing but many. First, it was a focal point of jazz history, representing the open meeting between Negro musicians and white musicians eager to learn. Out of this meeting came a couple of experimental offshoots towards new jazz, notably those of Teschemacher and Goodman. And out of this meeting came the development of what may be called a jazz scholarship, an almost scientific preservation of New Orleans and Dixieland qualities which the general forward movement of jazz had seemed to leave high and dry.

This monastic devotion to "pure" jazz gave rise to a cultist atmosphere among jazz followers which did little good to jazz and much harm. Musicians however, are not to be blamed for their disciples, critics and self-appointed theorizers. It was something admirable for a group of players to rise who played a jazz so consistently musical, cleancut and self-effacing, and gained adherents for hot as against commercial jazz.

These players also made progress, although in a specialized way. Except for Tesch they explored no new paths and created no new music of jazz. They saw great and important new developments arrive without taking part or showing much interest. But they moved towards a gradual recovery of forgotten qualities of the past. At first the music they played, after Teschemacher's death, tended to be excessively sweet. The solos and ensemble improvisations were bound within a handful of simple chords. They had the erroneous idea that the "Dixieland" style could be applied to any popular tunes, such as Gershwin's, by the simple expedient of ignoring the tune and improvising Dixieland solos over its chords; a practise which resulted in a still more saccharine music. They did not see that the handling of the pop tune really required, for musical value, the groundbreaking and imaginative approach of an Armstrong, Beiderbecke and Teschemacher. They did not even understand Dixieland, or New Orleans music; its interplay of solo and full band, its quality that I have described as "duet" or "concerto" style, its antiphonal and blues character. An example of the misreading of Dixieland music, although within its own limits it has some good spots, is Jimmy McPartland's performance of "Eccentric." A comparison to Spanier's masterly performance, with Cless and Brunis, is a lesson in true Dixieland style.

They learned, however. Joe Sullivan embarked on a broadening study of blues and rag piano, and evolved a brilliant, concentrated solo chorus style of real distinction. Kaminsky increased his expressive range so that, in latter years, he has been playing an outstandingly vibrant and powerful trumpet. Jack Teagarden's effortless outpouring of liquid blues melody was a great accession. Miff Mole plays today a much more blue and expressive trombone than in his Red Nichols recordings. The reappearance of Spanier after a spell of illness, with a band including Cless on clarinet and Brunis' genuine blues and tailgate trombone, during the late thirties, was a revelation of the true character of Dixieland music. Brunis, of course, was a New Orleans native and had been a member of the famous New Orleans Rhythm Kings, with Paul Mares and Leon Rappolo.

The change in style can be traced by comparing the first batch of records made by Condon's "Summa Cum Laude" band for Decca and Commodore, mostly a dull music, to the more recent, remarkable series on Commodore, built around Davison and Brunis, with Condon, Russell and Wettling of the old group. This is not mentioned to decry the talents of the older group, but to point up the general, all around improvement in understanding of the music. Another fine series was recorded by Blue Note with Art Hodes, Cless and Kaminsky, including some beautiful slow blues. A great advance was made in bringing Negro and white musicians together for performance. There has, as yet, not been a permanent group of Negro and white, however, the collaboration taking place in jam sessions and recording groups. This provided a more imaginative, humorous and poignant music. HRS made a notable series of records with "Pee Wee" Russell, Max Kaminsky, Zutty Singleton, Dickie Wells and

James P. Johnson, and another fine series featuring Sidney Bechet, Muggsy Spanier, Carmen Mastren on guitar and Wellman Braud on bass. Kaminsky, Bechet and Vic Dickenson produced some remarkable performances together. Edmond Hall, Cecil Scott and Albert Nicholas on clarinet, Sid Catlett on drums, were notable additions to many "Chicago," or what are now more properly described as "Dixieland" performances. Mezzrow and Bechet made a worthwhile series of records together.

"Chicago-Dixieland" music lacks the firm base in a broad audience, the excitement of fresh emotional experiences, that other modern jazz has attained. It is a music produced mostly for record collectors, and heard in a few night clubs, such as Nick's in New York, which have made a specialty of Chicago-style small bands. Yet it has a basis for life in the fact that the "new" jazz, for all its exciting advances, tends to be one-sided. It gained depth of emotional expression, a fine probing of subtle and personal moods, a biting irony, a breathtaking brilliance and surprise, but lost in relaxation, in breadth and solidity of form. This is not a commentary on the musicians who produced the music, but on the society which forced new creation to take place within such personal terms; which forced jazz, by the very pressures put upon it, into numerous, semi-private specializations. The harm comes when the problem is not seen correctly, and each path is advanced as the "whole" of jazz, or of the musical art. Chicago-Dixieland jazz offers nothing new, but preserves qualities of a past music that deserve to be remembered and cherished. It points the way to a time when our musical life will again provide, on a much broader scale than existed in New Orleans, opportunities for jazz to enter into people's lives; to take on broad and solid forms, with all the new richness of emotional expression modern jazz has made possible.

Teschemacher was the most original musical thinker produced by the Chicago group. Like Bix, he played a self-effacing, small-band, collective jazz, but made his great contribution as an individual personality, which impressed itself upon all the groups with which he worked. He rarely played a slow blues. Yet, as in the case of Bix, his style would have been impossible without New Orleans music and the blues. His clarinet timbre was reedy, with a deliberate avoidance of vibrato or any hint of sweetness. He developed the "blue" note into a solo and ensemble style, leaning heavily upon off-pitch notes. These are not handled in the tantalizing New Orleans manner of sliding on and off the pitch, or worrying a single note, but are struck solidly. In the ensembles he does not spin a line of decorative figures over a trumpet lead but, instead, strikes a blue note on the beat to give each chord a blue feeling, or else spins a series of short, staccato phrases which give a feeling of being in another key from the melodic lead. His solo melodic line wanders into strange keys without preparing the listener's ear. Instead they tantalize the ear with a feeling of being harmonically lost, but always return "home" in a satisfying way. These solos, entirely different from those of Bix in their brilliant and sardonic quality, are like Bix's tight, original, finely-constructed, musical organisms, built up to a fine climax in which he provides his own driving percussive lead and answering phrases.

There is an unrelaxed quality to Teschemacher's performances, and an unsatisfying all-over form. This is not due to any musical failure on his part, but rather to the fact that the other players were not thinking along his lines. The task he was coping with, like Beiderbecke and Armstrong, was that of making a creative music out of the popular tune, and his solos were triumphant strides in this direction, negating the over-sweetness of the pop tune with his soaring into the harmonic stratosphere.

Some commentators "explain" Tesch by claiming that he was simply a bad clarinet player, and couldn't play in tune. This is as foolish as the claim that Cezanne painted the way he did because he was near-sighted. Tesch used off-pitch notes as some modern composers use quarter-tones, to give the melodic line itself a plangent, strange and insecure quality. His solos, such as those on "There'll Be Some Changes Made," "Shim-me-sha-wobble," "Nobody's Sweetheart," "I Found a New Baby," "Oh Baby" (the latter employing alto sax and suffering from bad drumming), "Wailing Blues"; his surprise entrances and brilliant ensembles such as those in "China Boy"; all are the product of a calculating musical intelligence.

Much of the falling-off in admiration for Tesch was due to the unfruitful influence he had on others. This came about, however, only because, after his death,

"Chicago Style" was built around his work without understanding it. Tunes like "Nobody's Sweetheart," "Changes," "China Boy," were played as "Chicago" classics simply because Tesch had used them. Without his creative thinking the clarinet style modelled after Tesch produced neither good Dixieland nor good popular tune music. The blues were avoided because Tesch never seemed to use them directly. Solos became predominantly "on the beat" because that had been part of Tesch style. And so it was a great improvement for small Chicago-style outfits to rediscover the blues and real Dixieland, with the entrance of men like Hodes and Teagarden. We can see in the clarinet work of Cless and Russell a gradual return to Dixieland line. It was actually not towards a clarinet style but towards a tenor sax style that Teschemacher's work pointed. Bud Freeman, of all the Chicago boys, kept closest to the Tesch tradition, although he never produced as original a music. "Wailing Blues" and "Barrelhouse Stomp" show the Tesch influence, both on Bud and on the roughness of Wingy Mannone's fine trumpet. There is a close parallel between Tesch's work, as in "Shim-me-sha-wobble," and Coleman Hawkins' as in "Hello, Lola," and many solos in the Fletcher Henderson band. It is this writer's belief that, had Tesch and Bix both lived and continued to advance, they would have been playing music much like bebop. This is of course sheer speculation. The fact remains however that Tesch's music, although small in quantity and formal structure, is one of the contributions of jazz to permanent music.

Fletcher Henderson arrived at a musical compromise, similar to that of the Chicago groups, but from an opposite direction. Where the Chicago groups remained loyal to the small band, Henderson built a large-band style. Where the Chicago groups tended to minimize the actual musical content of Dixieland and New Orleans jazz, Henderson built up a repertory of rags, blues and stomps. His music remained, however, like that of the Chicago boys, weak in all-over form. It rested for its chief interest on the solos. Henderson, in his arrangements for large band, encountered a fundamental law that one change in any element of a musical texture, whether melody, harmony or instrumental timbre, requires a change in all. If a piano work or song is orchestrated, the music sounds worse rather than better, unless the orchestrator is daring enough to reconstruct the entire work in terms of the new musical sound, which makes the work almost a new composition. If a folk song is harmonized, something of its melodic character is lost, unless the musician really recreates the song into something new and fresh. If work for a single piano is played by two, four or six pianos, the resulting music is less rather than more effective.

Similarly, when we hear a blues line in Henderson's music played by two or three trumpets in unison instead of one, or by four reeds in harmony, the spontaneity is lost and nothing of importance, musically, is gained. The perfect economy of sound that makes the great New Orleans performance so complete and exciting a music in every detail is missing. Much of the character of the blues is lost. The two-line, antiphonal music dwindles down to one melodic line, often over-controlled and sweetened by the accompanying harmonies. The solos, even though, individually, each one is very fine, do not vary enough from one another and tend to neutralize each other's effect. The gathering monotony of a series of solos is intensified by the unchanging rhythmic pattern. The final climactic ensemble and ride-out is replaced by the band stating the theme in unison, or by a drivingly repeated riff.

High quality remains. Henderson did not choose the big band in order to impress anybody, nor did he in any way "commercialize" jazz music, a term sometimes loosely thrown about as if it were a crime for a musician to seek a fair return for his work. Henderson built a large band because such a band fitted the musical needs of the times. In his band he gave a host of fine musicians a chance to continue to play, to explore their instruments and the art of music, to make a living as musicians. His changing roster included such sterling instrumentalists as Tommy Ladnier, Joe Smith, Rex Stewart, Bobby Stark, Coleman Hawkins, Buster Bailey, Charley Green, Jimmy Harrisson, J. C. Higginbotham, Claude Jones, Dickie Wells, Keg Johnson, Roy Eldridge, Henry Allen, Leon

"Chu" Berry, John Kirby. Many of them are playing a beautiful, small-band jazz today, as are other "graduates" of Basie, Lunceford and Luis Russell. And Henderson began as well to explore the exciting new possibilities of the large band as a collective musical instrument.

He had a powerful influence on jazz, and for good. He brought the blues, rags and stomps, even in less than perfect form, to the attention of a public that had never heard this music before. He influenced the creation of large swing bands, such as Benny Goodman's, Bunny Berigan's, Tommy Dorsey's, Harry James', Charlie Barnett's and Woody Herman's, which also often played a blues and stomp music. The music of none of these makes a new contribution and has real permanence. But it is often forgotten, in criticizing the swing bands, that the public which listened to them would otherwise have been listening to Whiteman, Grofé, Kostelanetz and Kyser. The better swing bands introduced a new public to a music honestly orchestral, compelling in its sound, based on living folk material. "King Porter Stomp," "Sugarfoot Stomp," "One O'Clock Jump," "In the Mood," "Tuxedo Junction," were a far better music than the pretentions, imitation-symphony pastry offered by the general run of large dance bands, although they are not impressive to those who know the far better music from which they derive. Goodman's success sent a new host of listeners off to explore jazz. And he played a Henderson music, just as he, and the other bands, began also to play a Basie, Ellington, and even, in Berigan's case, an Armstrong and Bix music.

There is, furthermore, some very fine and original music on the Henderson records, although it is a music of fragments, of one or two startling solos in a performance. His great early groups lost their impact on recording because the old acoustic records couldn't begin to transmit the power of a twelve or fifteen piece band. A performance by a Henderson band, in "the flesh," was a far more thrilling experience than the records suggest. Yet, on the records, there are remarkable passages to be heard from Ladnier, Smith, Harrisson, Green, Stewart, and always Hawkins' rolling tenor sax, with its brilliant rhythmic patterns and contrast of long-drawn and staccato phrases.

The large band gave the Negro musician a new collective instrument to handle, with new riches of instrumental color, and dynamic contrasts. It provided the possibility for a new level of emotional expression, suited to the needs of a community that was living and thinking differently from that of New Orleans.

The large band, like the popular tune, brought to the musician a host of new problems; problems of chord sequences, of melody, of instrumental timbre and its relation to harmony, of musical form, of uniting on a higher level the individual contribution with the entire group. These problems had to be slowly and painfully worked out. For this reason Henderson's music may be called a transitional music. It is in Ellington's work that we can begin to see these problems solved.

RECORD ILLUSTRATIONS—CHAPTER FIVE

LOUIS ARMSTRONG—Solo Style

Knocking a Jug, Save it Pretty Mama, Squeeze Me (in Columbia Album C-28) West End Blues, Tight Like This, Muggles (in Columbia Album C-73) Stardust, Wrap Your Troubles in Dreams (Columbia Reissue) I Can't Give You Anything But Love (Columbia 38052) That's My Home (Victor 40-0102)

BIX BEIDERBECKE

Louisiana, Thou Swell, Goose Pimples, Old Man River (in Columbia Album C-29) Way Down Yonder in New Orleans, Clarinet Marmalade, Singing the Blues (in Columbia Album C-144) I'm Coming Virginia (Columbia 36280)

FRANK TESCHEMACHER

China Boy, Nobody's Sweetheart, Shim-me-sha-wobble, Oh Baby (in Columbia Album C-43) There'll Be Some Changes Made, I Found a New Baby, Wailing Blues, Barrelhouse Stomp (in Brunswick Album B-1017)

THOMAS "FATS" WALLER

Everybody Loves My Baby, Squeeze Me (Victor 20-2217) You're Not the Only Oyster in the Stew (Victor 20-2218) The Meanest Thing (Victor 20-2219) Honeysuckle Rose, Blues (A Jam Session at Victor) (Victor 25559)

FLETCHER HENDERSON

Money Blues, Stampede, Hop Off, Coming and Going, New King Porter Stomp, Snag It (in Columbia Album C-30)

Examples of the small Negro-white recording groups and of the Chicago-Dixieland music are not listed here, because outstanding examples have already been listed under other headings in previous chapters. They include the HRS records of "Pee Wee" Russell's Rhythmakers, the Bechet-Spanier Big Four, the Rex Stewart Big Seven and Jack Teagarden Big Eight; the Commodore series including "Wild" Bill Davison, George Brunis, Eddie

Condon, "Pee Wee" Russell, Max Kaminsky, Edmund Hall, Albert Nicholas, George Wettling and others; the various groups gotten together by Blue Note, including Art Hodes, Rod Cless, Sidney Bechet, Vic Dickenson, James P. Johnson, Max Kaminsky and others.

Fine Teagarden may be heard in the Brunswick Red Nichols album (Vol. 1, B 1001) and Columbia's "Comes Jazz" (C-40), although the surrounding performances are less inspired. He has a special flair for the nostalgic, semi-sweet blues song, such as "Aunt Hagar's Blues," "Yellow Dog Blues," "Basin Street Blues" (his fine recording of this with the Louisiana Rhythm Kings should be re-issued), "St. James Infirmary." His own original blues style ("Making Friends," Columbia 36010) is in similar character.

Most of the outstanding Bix solos are found on available records, but there should be some method of concentrating on a few records the fine little choruses and half choruses scattered through many otherwise worthless records. Tesch is almost completely represented on available records.

CHAPTER SIX

THE EXPERIMENTAL LABORA-
TORY AND THE NEW JAZZ . . .

t was Edward Kennedy "Duke" Ellington who established jazz in the mind of
every serious music student as an important music in its own right, needing
no "popular" qualifications. After his
work became known, jazz became impossible to ignore.
In its handling of instrumental sound, in its power of
melody, in its rightness of harmony and interweaving of
melodic lines, it met every specification of good music
within its small scope, and made many products of the
conservatories seem, by comparison, mechanical and
bloodless. Jazz was music, and the fact that it was also
music of dance and song, that it was of the people in
idiom and form, only opened up new and challenging
ideas as to how good music really came into being.

This does not mean that Ellington's music was better than any jazz that had come before, or was even the best jazz of its time. It does not even mean that Ellington was wholly understood by those who praised him. Ellington's music was not "better" than New Orleans music. It was good for Ellington's time as New Orleans had been for its own time. Ellington used musical materials that were familiar to concert trained ears, making jazz music more listenable to them. These however do not account for his real quality. He even did some harm to jazz, although not of any permanent nature, by falling into the subtle self-deprecation, forced upon members of a minority people who rise in the commercial entertainment world. We have already seen this happening in some of Armstrong's performances. Thus the "jungle" titles Ellington gave to some of his earlier works fostered a wrong characterization of both himself and jazz. The works so described were generally mixtures of blues and sweet, mountain folk song, like the beautiful "Echoes of the Jungle." Ellington of course has fought his way out of this kind of publicity, and so a later blues work of his, very much like "Echoes of the Jungle," is given the far more meaningful title, "Across the Track."

Ellington's work is in the main line of jazz. Comparisons of "better" or "worse," between works of one period and those of another, are meaningless and confusing. The struggle in art is to remain good. The world moves, and art must change. The problem of the creative artist is to do for his own time, for his own audiences, what the best achievements of the past did for their own times. This means the avoidance of meaningless repetitions of old patterns that have served their purpose. It means a constant awareness of new human and musical problems and a struggle to solve them.

This is Ellington's achievement. In his work all the elements of the old music may be found, but each completely changed, because it had to be changed. He may be called a kind of Haydn of jazz, reconstructing all the old materials of jazz in terms of the new sound demanded by his times, as Haydn brought together elements from folk song, comic opera, serenade and street music and infused them into the budding symphony.

His records, taken singly, are not obviously better than other single performances of the time. He produced, however, the most consistent stream of first-rate jazz over a period of more than fifteen years; and this was due to his ability to restore, in terms of the new conditions he had to face, something of the social character of New Orleans music. He gave jazz, in a limited way, a kind of permanent home, in which it could enjoy a degree of security and still continue to experiment. He provided, at least within the confines of his own band, an opportunity for communal music making, and on a higher technical level than had been possible in the past. At the same time, owning a keen musical curiosity and a deep personal integrity, he insisted on the right to change his music whenever he saw fit, regardless of commercial demands. It was an achievement for him to build up so phenomenal a band as he did, and hold its core together over so long a period of time. It was an achievement for him to avoid the morass of tin-pan-alley song plugging, or the blind alley of a successful "style" and remaining holed up in it. Thus he grew as a musician, and gave his fine, creative instrumentalists likewise a chance to grow.

Ellington's accomplishment was to solve the problem of form and content for the large band. He did it not by trying to play a pure New Orleans blues and stomp music, rearranged for large band, as Henderson did, but by recreating all the elements of New Orleans music in new instrumental and harmonic terms. What emerged was a music that could be traced back to the old roots and yet sounded fresh and new. Many jazz commentators, noticing how different Ellington's music sounded from the old jazz, concluded that he had made a complete break with it. The truth is the opposite. It was because he was faithful to the essential character of the old music that his music sounded different. Experiment is, itself, a characteristic of the old jazz. If present day Dixieland performances reproduce beautifully the actual sound of the old music, Ellington continues its defiance of set patterns, its constant welcoming and absorption of new ideas, its unpredictable twists and turns.

He made the large band, of three trumpets, three trombones, four or five reeds and a four-man rhythm sec-

tion as flexible, subtle and strong a music instrument as
the old seven piece band, capable of the most delicate
shades of tone and the most blasting power. This was an
achievement not of mechanical instrumental knowledge,
but a knowledge of harmony, and mastery of the musical problem of the relation of harmony to instrumental
timbre. What is unique in Ellington's instrumental sense,
compared to that of other large band arrangers, is his
realization that instrumental timbre is itself a part of
harmony, and harmony must be understood in terms of
timbre. Such an appreciation of harmony takes into con-
sideration not only the tones directly produced by the
instruments, but also the overtones. These overtones, the
faintly heard tones that mix with the struck tone to produce the characteristic color or timbre of an instrument,
are real tones that have their place in the musical scale.
Ellington built his chords on the understanding that
when two or three instruments perform together, their
overtones also combine, along with the notes directly
played, and either strengthen or muddy the resulting
harmony. In other words, a chord played by clarinet,
trumpet and trombone together, as in "Mood Indigo," is
quite different from the same chord sounded on the
piano. In "Mood Indigo" Ellington even added to his
conscious musical thinking the microphone tone produced by the three combined instruments. Among his
recent experiments in timbre has been the use of Kay

Davis' wordless singing, in "Minnehaha," and "On a Turquoise Cloud."

Ellington's use of rich chord and sound effects has been assailed by jazz purists as imitating romantic or impressionist composed music. There is something laughable in their easy slinging about of names like Debussy, or Delius, as if comparison to such masters were insulting. There would be some point to the criticism if Ellington had merely borrowed from these composers, as is sometimes done by tin-pan-alley arrangers and song manufacturers. The proof of Ellington's quality lies in the force of the music itself. It sounds exactly like no music written in Europe or anywhere else. It speaks a language of its own. It has been imitated, even by European composers, far more than it has imitated anybody. The real parallel is that Ellington was working independently, and within the harrowing limitations placed upon a band leader in the cut-throat, business entertainment world, upon problems similar to those being worked upon by European composers. His achievements in orchestral sound, timbre and harmonic relations, are an addition to musical knowledge.

Ellington created not only a new sound for the large band, but also a new idiom for it; an idiom drawn partly out of the blues, partly out of popular ballad. The blues are generally the familiar, basic twelve-bar blues, but harmonically more adventurous, adding new, "dissonant" intervals to the familiar, basic, blues chords, and new chromatic notes, but giving the improvising musician the same concentrated, emotional phrases, the same ability to build a musical structure out of them, the same freedom to soar without regard for traditional diatonic harmony, as in the past. In other words, Ellington preserved the harmonic character of the blues, but developed them melodically. What he did with the popular ballad idiom was just as right, and exactly the opposite. He dropped the melodic line, which was generally meaningless, and developed the diatonic and chromatic harmonies that had entered jazz with the popular ballad, creating his own far more sinuous and interesting melody.

The blues can be traced throughout Ellington's music. They are sometimes over-sweet, as in "Bundle of Blues," but also often wilder, accenting blue and non-diatonic notes more forcefully. Typical of Ellington's use of the blues are the following, taken from most of his recording career: "The Mooche," "Saratoga Swing," "Baby When You Ain't There," "Clarinet Lament," "Echoes of Harlem," "Mobile Bay," "Things Ain't What They Used To Be," "A Portrait of Bert Williams," "Jack the Bear," "Across the Track," "Cotton Tail," "Carnegie Blues" (from "Black, Brown and Beige"). These are an education in the manner in which the blues can be made the germ for the greatest variety of melodic patterns, each with its own mood.

New Orleans music, as I have shown, was not a pure blues music but boasted a variety of musical languages, achieving its finest music in an interplay of blues with one or another idiom, "hot" and "sweet." This became a basic characteristic of Ellington's music. "Black and Tan Fantasy" for example was based on a New Orleans tune much like Oliver's "Chimes Blues" and "Canal Street Blues," with a touch of Chopin's funeral march. "East St. Louis Toodle-oo" is based on a minor-key lament like "St. James Infirmary" or Armstrong's "Tight Like This." He often used many of the sweeter and mountain-inspired folk songs, such as those which open "Rocky Mountain Blues," "Big House Blues," "Saturday Night Function," "Echoes of the Jungle," "Saratoga Swing." He used chromatic, Spanish, mock-oriental and Cuban melodic lines, as in "Mood Indigo," "Boy Meets Horn," "The Mooche," "Caravan," "Rocking in Rhythm," "Koko" and "Conga Brava," playing these idioms in all cases against a straight blues.

Not only did Ellington preserve the melodic curve of the blues, but he also preserved the antiphonal, two-voiced character of the blues, so important in preventing their degeneration into over-sweetness. One rarely hears in his music a single, sustained, melodic line, or a simple, unbroken series of riffs. There is always the antiphony, the statement and answer, found in the interplay of the solo instrument against the full band, of one instrument in dialogue with another, of brass choir against reeds. Even when the solo instrument holds the scene for a series of choruses, its solo lines are of the two-voiced character.

Bigard and Hodges are masters at this kind of blues line. Ellington's style and method of construction are generally based on the antiphonal contrast, duet or "concerto" style, starting within the basic themes themselves and characterizing the entire performance.

This method has enabled Ellington to make the fullest use of the creative talents of his performers, allowing them to grow as individual masters of their instruments and as composers. Ellington's music is fundamentally his own, shaped by his taste and musical thinking. Yet, within these bounds, the complete performance is a kind of collective creation restoring, within the narrow confines of a single band, the social character of New Orleans music. Other large bands depended heavily upon solo improvisations. The Duke, however, evolved a most subtle and inventive musical style, which could set the character of an entire performance, give the soloist short phrases upon which to improvise, and provide a most inventive harmonic and instrumental backing to bring out the best in the solo. The soloist finds complete freedom to develop the possibilities of his instrument, and his creative musical ideas. The performance is relaxed, the soloist only speaking when he has something to say.

Thus Ellington's music has remained his own, and yet changed its character with the entrance or departure of outstanding soloists. The soloists profit by learning from one another, often taking off from another's style and developing their own, as "Cootie" Williams absorbed

Miley. There is a double line of development to the music, that of Ellington and that of the character brought by the outstanding instrumentalists. "Bubber" Miley's growl and "wa-wa" tones on the early records, like "Black and Tan," "Got Everything But You," "Jubilee Stomp," are legendary, as well as his poignant blues and minor key, melodic lines. Williams went even further in transforming this roughness into the most sensuous beauty, as in "Echoes of Harlem" or "Delta Mood" and expanding it to the full range of the instrument, as in "Concerto for Cootie." Rex Stewart mixed together plunger, half-valve, muted tones, open-horn tones heavily blued, and the cloudy lower register, as in "Boy Meets Horn," "Bragging in Brass," "Mobile Bay" and "Dusk."

When the clarinet tended to die out elsewhere as a major large band instrument, Ellington made a most consistently effective use of the instrument. He was aided, of course, by having a man like Barney Bigard, so deeply rooted in the blues idiom and yet so inventive in fresh melodic lines and so masterly in technique. Examples run through all of Ellington's work, a few being "Saratoga Swing," "Clarinet Lament," "Jack the Bear," the joyous small band "Caravan," "Minuet in Blues," "Mood Indigo." With trombone men like "Tricky" Sam Nanton, exploiting the growl tones, Juan Tizol the sweetness and staccato sharpness of the valve trombone, Lawrence Brown playing a Teagarden-like gentle and lyrical line and tone, but always with an expressive burr, Ellington explored about everything that could be done with the instrument short of J. J. Johnson's bebop style. Examples are "Ducky Wucky," "Black and Tan Fantasy," "Caravan" and "Bragging in Brass." With Johnny Hodges he made a major instrument of the alto saxophone, and brought into being perhaps the finest body of alto sax music in the history of jazz. The fullest range of tone and timbre is exploited, from the blues of "The Mooche," "Saratoga Swing," "Dooji Wooji," "Wanderlust," "Things Ain't What they Used to Be," to the chromatic, ballad-like lyricism of "Warm Valley." Hodges also created, with the exception of Bechet, and in a style of his own, probably the most beautiful soprano sax music on records. The work of Harry Carney, of course, on baritone sax, is legendary, and runs throughout Ellington's recorded output, a fine example being the small-band "Caravan." Ben Webster inspired some fine compositions using the tenor sax, such as "Conga Brava," "Sepia Panorama," "Just a Settin' and a Rockin' " and the amazing "Cotton Tail." With Sonny Greer on drums, Fred Guy on guitar and himself on piano, Wellman Braud and Jimmy Blanton on bass, Ellington had a masterly rhythm section of which he made prolific use. Braud's slapping bass, unaided, cut through the orchestral sound with powerful effect, as in "Saturday Night Function" or "Beggar's Blues." Blanton developed a solo style of great tonal beauty and power, as in "Jack the Bear" and "Ko Ko." Ellington's piano is sustained and chordal rather than percussive, and melodic, and provides a most beautiful punctuation of a solo melodic line. Perhaps the most amazing rhythmic achievement, among many, is "Cotton Tail," in which bass, piano and drums play a remarkable individual role, and at the climax the entire band beats out a brilliant two-rhythm pattern.

Ellington's forms are simple in outline, yet fitting perfectly the demands of unity and variety. The form he most often uses may be described as A-B-A. "A" stands for the opening theme, which is actually a group of two or three melodies, and is antiphonal from the very first bars. It is repeated, but the repetition is interestingly varied, the statement the same but the solo answer different. "B" is a contrasting middle section, frequently the section where the blues enter, often treated as a series of solos or duets. Then "A" returns, but always on a new harmonic twist, a cadence or instrumental reply, rounding out the performance like the classical "coda."

The old stomp, rag and slow-blues forms often return within this framework, although so changed that they are apparent only as the skeleton of the music. "Bragging in Brass," for example, is a brilliant take-off on "Tiger Rag." The riff is an important element in this form, and never repeated to the point of monotony. It sometimes forms the opening band phrases, answered by the solo instrument; sometimes the band accompaniment to the solos; sometimes the means through which the orchestra re-enters after a solo chorus. Some of the most interesting examples of the use of the riff are "East St. Louis Toodle-oo," "Diminuendo in Blue," "Good Gal Blues," "Just a Settin' and a Rockin'," "Concerto for Cootie." An important factor in the Duke's progress has been the experimentation often carried on in smaller band units. Some of his most beautiful records are those made under the names of his bandsmen, such as Barney Bigard, "Cootie" Williams, Rex Stewart, and Sonny Greer. In these records his new musical ideas are distilled down to the smallest group of instrumentalists that can handle them, often resembling the old New Orleans combinations. During the period when the sweeter, more "symphonic" records were considered the hall-mark of his style, the Duke addressed these hotter, small-group records to a more knowing, proletarian audience.

Although the records employing singers and popular songs are among the less interesting, even these have great distinction compared to the work of the other, song-plugging bands of the time. The vocal sections are not merely a sung chorus, but part of a vocal-instrumental form that has a beginning, middle and end, and an interesting, constantly changing timbre. More often the Duke has made up his own songs, replacing the over-sweet, harmonically confined, tin-pan-alley ballad with a chromatic and sinuously moving melodic line; and he has made this kind of melodic line the basis as well for a number of large-band compositions. Frequently this diatonic and chromatic melodic line will combine with the blues, to produce a polytonal music of two different keys or musical systems used at the same time. "Cotton Tail" based on the blues, is a remarkable example, of a richly harmonized, polytonal music. "Ko Ko" is another interesting example of harmonic boldness, using definite modulations or key changes and definite polytonal passages, yet with the music always lucid, under control and rounded out. These performances lead directly into bebop.

Ellington's career led him to cope with the musical problem of the tin-pan-alley ballad, and its accompanying harmonic system. Great experimentation was needed to solve this problem. For a time, when the Duke moved away from the blues and folk-inspired music of his earlier period to such richer-sounding, sweetly harmonized works as "Reminiscing in Tempo," or partially successful experiments in dissonance as "Crescendo in Blue" and "Diminuendo in Blue," it was thought that he was slipping backward. But this was a necessary germination period, out of which came the magnificent Victor series of the late 'thirties, where the blues return in full force but completely changed, the harmonies are freed from the tin-pan-alley straightjacket, the form is immaculate in its unity.

His influence was considerable upon the general run of popular band music, and for good. Fletcher Henderson used his style in such performances as "Hot and Anxious" and "Coming and Going," Charlie Barnet in many rearrangements of Ellington works and original conceptions,

Benny Goodman in performances of Ellington works, Louis Armstrong, Bob Crosby, Woody Herman, Benny Carter, Will Hudson, Artie Shaw, Jimmie Lunceford, Eddie Sauter, Raymond Scott. A great many "tone poems," riff compositions, atmosphere and "mood" pieces were inspired by Ellington. They are largely worthless as permanent music, often representing only the commercially inspired practise of duplicating in innumerable copies every stylistic device invented by creative jazz. But still, within this process, we find creative jazz raising the level of musical performance. Impermanent as these jazz compositions are, it is an advance for people to be listening to an orchestral music actually conceived in instrumental terms, and to a harmonic system as fresh and exciting as often enters into these works. It may be that, as jazz continues to advance, many of Ellington's records will have lost their interest. But there will be a core of about fifty records that are enduring contributions to jazz and American music. Over and above this contribution, Ellington's career is that of a man who has been an educative force in all of American music. Typical of the contributions that jazz has continually made to American life, this has been the product of a self-educated musician, struggling with some of the most abstruse problems of music under the most prohibitive conditions.

Ellington's latest move has been into the concert field, with works such as "Black, Brown and Beige" and

"Liberia Suite." These will be discussed in the next chapter. However, it can be said here that they mark another advance. If this step is not carried forward to its completion, it will not be Ellington's fault. Rather it will be a result of the same contradiction that has plagued jazz from its New Orleans beginnings; the awareness by jazz musicians of solutions to new problems, which the miserable cultural life in which they have to work prevents them from realizing.

Bill Basie, called the "Count," brought to jazz a style and body of music less varied than Ellington's, but one deeply rooted in folk art, powerful in its influence on jazz up to and including bebop. Much of the power of his band and of its influence came, of course, from its individual performers. These included, at various times, such outstanding musicians as Shad Collins, Harry Edison and Buck Clayton on trumpet, Hershel Evans, Lester Young and Tab Smith on sax, Dickie Wells and Bennie Morton on trombone, a phenomenal rhythm section consisting of Basie himself on piano, Joe Jones on drums, Walter Page on bass and Freddie Green on guitar. Each of the above is a remarkable performer, both in his handling of the instrument and the solid quality of his musical ideas.

The music offered by the Basie band was founded on blues of the sweeter, mellow and folkish kind, reminiscent of old spirituals, and mountain dances, often in or suggesting a minor key. This kind of melody defines, as well as anything, the essential character of Kansas City jazz, for it is heard not only in Basie but in the fine piano pieces and arrangements of Mary Lou Williams, and in the blues piano of Pete Johnson. His forms were based on the riff, which he used with the greatest subtlety. Unlike some later, large-band mechanizations of the riff, the Basie performances used the riff, and its solo reply or obbligato, in a manner based on old choral spirituals. The "jump" rhythm, as he used it, also comes from a spirituals background, and in his hands it always has the human elasticity which it lacks in a manneristic treatment.

Instrumentally, Basie was strong in the one point where Ellington had been comparatively weak. Ellington had never made much of the solo tenor sax; a condition only partially remedied by the arrival of Ben Webster and Al Sears. The tenor sax became the leading solo instrument in the Basie band, and the other instruments tended to develop a tone and melodic style to parallel the sax. And so one hears a great deal of muted trumpet from Edison, Clayton and Collins, the tone sustained and given subtle, sax-like inflections. A somewhat similar style was worked out independently by Frankie Newton. The trombone likewise developed a new style, wholly different from the explosive "tailgate." It spins out sustained melodic lines, depending for their effect upon the beauty of the melody itself, and upon its sudden twists and surprises, with a hint of the presence of two voices. Even the rhythm section developed a kind of singing style. Joe Jones gave the band a powerful, underlying beat, but the actual sound of the drums, merged with the string tone of Green's guitar and Page's bass, took on a juicy sound. We become conscious of the actual presence of the drums only in the very free, economical punctuations of the solos and the riffs. Jones' teamwork with Lester Young or Dickie Wells, in which he seems to read their minds, is always a thing of beauty. Basie's own piano style was similarly new, and similarly singing. It exploited mainly the right hand, which would reiterate a riff almost to the breaking point, and then, by delightful contrast, lay out a melody with widely spaced notes or chords. The left hand entered with sudden, surprise chords, punctuating the right hand melodic line, or suggesting the entrance of a "congregation" or chorus.

A good idea of the basic style of Kansas City melody can be gotten from the following records: "Topsy" by the Basie band, which in a half-serious, half-humorous way pictures a revival meeting; James Rushing's singing of "Sent for You Yesterday" with the band; "Roll 'em Pete" with Pete Johnson and Joe Turner; Mary Lou Williams' "Harmony Blues"; Andy Kirk's "Twinkling," featuring Mary Lou Williams, and "Floyd's Guitar Blues," featuring Floyd Smith; Leroy Carr's "How Long, How Long Blues" and "When the Sun Goes Down" given very beautiful performances by Basie's piano accompanied by the rhythm section; Pete Johnson's "You Don't Know My Mind," "Pete's Blues," "Kaycee on My Mind." This music has its emotional limitations. It cannot represent the whole of jazz. But it belongs with the most full-throated, singing music in jazz, an imperishable addition to the knowledge we have of our riches of folk song. Like New Orleans music, it proves that jazz is not a style, but a music from which the style derives. "Kansas City Jazz" is such a music.

Like every other style derived from jazz music, Kansas City and the Basie style have become mannerisms of commercial and semi-commercial music. A great mass of the large, swing-band music drew upon the Basie use of riffs, solos, and jump beat. The riffs provided an easy solution of structural or "composition" problems. The improvisation within the chords, suggested by the riffs, provided an easy way of playing "hot." The jump beat, a four-to-the-bar pattern with two sharply accented, and slightly delayed off-beats, actually two diametrically opposed rhythmic patterns, gives each bar a frenetic excitement which leaves an impression of something very stirring going on. But there is a great difference between the best Basie music and the swing band repetitions of it.

Basie's use of the riff is sensitively musical. "One O'Clock Jump" is an example, starting with Basie's piano and Morton's trombone, then building up to its full band, riff climax. It is a fine piece of music, although it has been dinned into our ears so much by every large band that it has become hard to listen to with unbiased mind. "Taxi War Dance," "Jump for Me," "Swinging the Blues," "Panassie Stomp," are other good riff compositions. Another characteristic of Basie is that the riffs are varied throughout the performances; still another that they are, in themselves, melodies of great beauty. The riffs of "One O'Clock Jump," "Jump for Me," "Swinging the Blues," have become part of the folk lore of swing music.

As for the jump beat, it was handled by the Basie band with the utmost elasticity, so that the solos are not in the least bound by it, but rather supported, as a base from which to soar. This is not the case with mechanical jump music, where the initial excitement given by the beat soon passes into monotony.

Lastly the solos themselves are no bare "noodling" of a chord, but are themselves melodic lines of real and lasting power. Lester Young has made the outstanding contribution to this kind of solo music, but it is noticeable that in the Basie performances, he rarely overbalances the others. There seems to be a fine interchange of ideas between him and Edison, Wells, Clayton, Collins, and Evans, so that all the solos stand up as music and all sound born out of the same musical source.

Of Basie's band music, as of many other jazz contributors, it is possible to say that the greatest work is the early work. Sometimes this attitude is an indication only of critical laziness—praise of the music most familiar to us. In many cases, however, there is a real falling off. The reason is again the business-run, unmusical atmosphere of our entertainment world. Good music cannot be

a short order product. It has a slow germination; an achievement should be respected and preserved until it is superseded by another work equally good. In the world Basie entered, however, any new contribution was immediately taken up and often so vulgarized as to become trite. The drive for continual novelty, without providing the conditions or the desire for the really new, resulted in superficiality. Works like the two-part "Miss Thing," and the accompaniment to Paul Robeson singing "King Joe," indicate how solid a large-band music Basie might have developed. Such a contribution, however, depends not only on a Basie, but on the conditions under which he has to work. If a band such as Ellington's or Basie's were made a national or local concern, given a steady, relaxed existence, removed from the terrible insecurity and homelessness that afflicts a band musician's life, and encouraged to develop its own music, the results would be astounding. The story of jazz is not only the history of a great created music, but also the tragedy of a potentially great, never-created music.

If Basie's influence upon large-band jazz was a fruitful one, his influence upon small--band jazz was even more far-reaching. It is unwise, in discussions of jazz, to trace direct influences from one figure to another. Such relationships are easy to draw on paper, but don't generally correspond to the more complex facts. Yet Basie's music was certainly one of the chief factors in the formation of the new kind of small-band music, wholly different from New Orleans and Dixieland style.

Basie's own piano style indicates the base for this music. It employs the full piano, but uses rich chords and full sounds sparingly, to punctuate and support the solo melodic lines. His large-band music also has this character, the full band often heard in many performances only for punctuation. "Blue and Sentimental," "Dogging Around," "Twelfth St. Rag," the full-band "Lady Be Good," are examples of this large-band style which has the feeling of a small band. It was easy to move from this kind of music to an actual small-band music. A single trumpet, trombone and sax, if used together with a good knowledge of harmony, could sound chords as solid as a full-band choir. A single instrument, such as Basie's piano or Young's tenor, could riff as effectively as, and even more subtly than, a full band or full choir.

And so a small-band music came into being based on rich harmonized sounds, a combination of harmony and instrumental texture, the jump beat, the riff, the solo. Basie developed such a music in the "Jones-Smith" records, and those under the name of the "Kansas City Six" and "Seven." We can see the change to a new kind of small-band music take place in Goodman, always the intelligent absorber of new trends. In his first trio and quartet records, with Teddy Wilson, Gene Krupa, and Lionel Hampton, he plays a refinement of Dixieland style. In records like "Pick-a-rib" he shows the transition

to the riff style, which then dominates his sextet performances. Aiding in the latter were Basie himself, in some
performances, "Cootie" Williams, George Auld and the
great Charlie Christian on the guitar.

An interesting parallel may be observed here to
European composed music. In the later nineteenth century, after the death of Haydn, Beethoven and Schubert,
the symphonic concert hall tended toward showy, trivial
virtuoso music. This led the serious composers to put
their deepest thoughts into chamber music. Brahms is
outstanding among those whose chamber music absorbed
many harmonic and dynamic ideas from the symphony,
even creating a symphonic kind of music for the violin
and piano sonata. In our own century we find Schoenberg
reducing the harmonic and instrumental texture of Wagner's operatic writing down to a few instruments.

The parallel to jazz is not accidental. In both cases
the avenues through which the artist can reach the
largest public, and use the most ambitious forms are vir-
tually shut to the honest musician. The concert hall was
taken over by an upper class consisting of the declining
aristocracy and its imitators among the newly rich; in its
latest development it has become an adjunct of radio and
recording chains. The large jazz band is also bound to
the increasingly monopolized, musical entertainment system. The small group remains the place where the musician can work out his most sincere ideas; but the price
he pays for this limited freedom is bare living, insecurity,

and isolation from the public for whom he should be working.

It is this isolation that dominates the production of most modern jazz. It is a small-band music created mainly for musicians. This does not mean that the players disdain a larger audience, or that large audiences, when they get to know the music, do not enjoy it. There are no real operating relations, however, between the musician and the public. The public is limited in its choice to what radio and record company offer. The musician does not face a public he can respond to. The "public" to him is represented by the band manager, the agent who negotiates the recording date, the company official, the publicity man; everybody but the actual people for whom he should be playing.

This isolation has had its psychological effect upon jazz. It has given rise to cults. It has caused performers, sometimes, to turn to stimulants and narcotics, with their eventual ruin as musicians. In some modern jazz it has caused an experiment for experiment's sake, a personal probing of new chord constructions and sequences, as a rebellion against the music that the prevalent practise forces upon the musician. These provide some ideas for new music, but they cannot be the new music itself.

With the exception of Ellington's music, most modern jazz has evolved in an experimental laboratory consisting mainly of groups of players from large bands who worked out new ideas in privacy. Many experimental players found a home, long-term or temporary, in Jimmy Lunceford's band, Cab Calloway's, Earl Hines', Woody Herman's and Billy Eckstein's. Some small groups, like John Kirby's band or the King Cole trio, have been commercially successful but not with their best music. Many players today perform in "sweet" style in public life, and in fine hot style with small jam session groups. An example is the fine work of "King" Cole, on piano, and Les Paul, on guitar, in volumes four and seven of "Jazz at the Philharmonic."

Small groups which served as the experimental laboratories were Jimmie Noone's Apex Club band, with Earl Hines, back in the late '20's; the Benny Goodman trio, quartet, quintet and sextet; the various groups which Teddy Wilson, Billie Holiday and Frankie Newton gathered for recording purposes. Many of these groups and sessions did not produce a music of absolute, lasting power. Yet they played a music far above the commercial music being heard at the time and, at the same time, avoided the "purist" repetition of Dixieland patterns. They broke new ground.

They often suffered from excessive harmonic sweetness, over-dependence on riffing for structure, or from instrumental brilliance for its own sake. This was a necessary avenue to progress, however, for the job they tackled was the exploration of the full tonal possibilities of the instrument, and the absorption of the popular ballad. When this was accomplished, as it is in much modern jazz and bebop, virtuosity for its own sake could be thrown away, leaving only skill in execution, and the popular ballad could be discarded, leaving only the new harmonic system and ideas that developed out of it.

Many of the records made by these groups are alive today. Some of the earlier Goodman records, like "Someday Sweetheart," "Where or When," "Sweet Lorraine," "I Know that You Know," are enjoyable, with Wilson's piano fresh and fanciful. Some of the Holiday records, such as "I Wished on the Moon" and "What a Little Moonlight Can Do," have not only Holiday's finer singing but enjoyable work by Goodman and Eldridge. Another group of Holiday's records enlist the services of Basie's men, notably Lester Young, as in "Back in Your Own Back Yard," "I Can't Get Started," "Easy Living," "The Very Thought of You," "When You're Smiling," "The Man I Love." The Goodman sextet performances, with Christian, "Cootie" Williams, Auld and Basie, are memorable. "Red" Norvo and his "selected sextet," including Teddy Wilson, Charlie Parker, John "Dizzy" Gillespie, "Slam" Stewart, "Flip" Phillips and J. C. Heard made a group of sides for Comet, "Congo Blues," "Get Happy," "Slam Slam Blues," and "Hallelujah," in which the qualities of bebop are heard, full blown.

Records have helped bring musicians and public partly together, for the record-buyers are generally more discriminating than heterogeneous theatre audiences. Particularly the smaller record companies, some of them operating on a shoe-string, have tried to take up where the large companies leave off, and record the better music that the musicians can play but the public can rarely hear. But this is no adequate solution. The small companies must also make money, and produce records that are strictly or semi-commercial, in performances often haphazard and insufficiently rehearsed.

Some record producers operate on the "genius" theory of jazz, according to which jazz is the creation of individual "geniuses" who mysteriously think up a "new music"; and so a great performance is to be achieved simply by throwing a group of these "geniuses" together. Or at the other extreme, the record sponsor thinks of himself as a "genius," or at least an Ellington, and ruins the music with his own interference. Nothing is further from the truth. Jazz is predominantly a social music. The jazz performer doesn't want to be known as a "genius," but wants mainly to play the music that satisfies him, to find an audience interested in listening, to get a decent wage for performing it, and a decent home life and security. He does his best work with others, and for interested people.

To make good records is not easy. The sponsor must represent the audience and provide, in his own appreciation of the best music, the contagion of a living audience. He must select men who work well together; he must use musical ideas that the men have worked over, or feel they can work with. He must be interested in good

music, rather than publicizing himself. He must provide
time for rehearsal, or for some working out of the best
possible use of the ideas.

To find good, live performances is also not easy.
Except for such progressive steps as Norman Granz's
"Jazz at the Philharmonic" series, and some of the jam
sessions, jazz club and Town Hall concerts in New York,
jazz is heard either as part of a pretentious stage show in
a movie house, or in a night club, where it remains, as
Eddie Condon calls it, a "poor man's music that only the
rich can afford."

The characteristics of modern jazz, including bebop,
are the use of forms based on riffs, with solo elaborations
on the chords implied in the riffs; the development of
the jam session, encouraging the soloist to build his own
musical structure out of a series of choruses; the intensification of rhythm; the absorption of the popular tune,
and the development of its diatonic idiom into "strange"
chords such as ninths and elevenths, familiar chords diminished or augmented, the use of chromatic notes, and
free and continual change of key; the exploration of the
extreme registers of the solo instrument; the reappearance
of the blues, as a part of the new harmonic writing.

The line out of Kansas City music can be easily
traced in a series of records. We can start with Basie's
"Topsy," a work that has reappeared under different
names. Leon "Chu" Berry's "Maelstrom," made with
Cab Calloway's band, carries a similar, minor-key, blues

riff a step further. The Kansas City Seven's "Destination K. C.," with a small Basie group, is again in the same pattern, with freer solos. Coleman Hawkins' "Ladies' Lullaby," made with a small group including Howard McGhee, carries the same kind of music onward. Gillespie's "Good Bait" is a workable cross between straight Kansas City and bebop music. Finally Gillespie's "One Bass Hit" and "Emmanon" carry the same procedure directly into the harmonic and rhythmic stratosphere of bebop. Even "Things to Come" is of the same pattern, although the Kansas City roots are heavily covered over.

The expansion of instrumental tone and technique took two forms; the refinement of collective tone, and the elaboration of the solo instrument. Both advanced together. In the Benny Goodman small-band records, from the first trio performances, through "Vibraphone Blues" with Lionel Hampton and the sextet's "Air Mail Special," and "As Long as I Live" we may see the subtle matching of timbres, the neat economy and control of the solos, the finesse of the rhythm. A major instrument, in modern jazz, is the tenor saxophone. Coleman Hawkins and "Chu" Berry led in giving the instrument a solid, unsentimental tone capable of the utmost refinement and the most impressive power, using it for subtle inflections of a melodic line and brilliant, rapid and staccato figurations. Illinois Jacquet is another tenor sax powerhouse, making a mannerism of the lowest honking tones and the highest screaming ones, but also capable of handling its middle registers with mastery. Charlie Parker made the alto sax an instrument of blinding technical brilliance, sometimes expressively sweet in tone but never saccharine, weaving melodic lines full of musical as well as technical surprises.

On trumpet and trombone the instrumental advances are less impressive, mainly due to the fact that New Orleans music, and its derivations, had exploited these instruments so fully. After Louis Armstrong, Lee Collins, "Cootie" Williams, Rex Stewart, "Kid" Ory, J. C. Higginbotham, Vic Dickenson, Sandy Williams, Jack Teagarden, Lawrence Brown, it is hard to see what more can be done with these instruments. The movement on trumpet was mainly towards the higher reaches of the instrument, partly for virtuoso display but also because the saxes filled in so much of the middle registers of the music. Henry Allen and Roy Eldridge worked out of Armstrong's style into an exploitation of high notes and fast runs, dominated by a jump beat. Charlie Shavers and Howard McGhee developed brilliant melodic styles using the higher notes, and Gillespie, of course, set himself the challenge of playing faster than anybody had ever done before. The trombone took itself a more modest tonal and technical role, the "new" style in the hands of "Trummy" Young and J. J. Johnson being one of fluid movement into strange intervals and modulations.

Art Tatum on the piano brought concert-hall technique to jazz. Earl Hines' brilliant suspended rhythms and harmonic curiosity fitted directly into the new jazz. On guitar the main innovation was the use of the electric instrument, which could cut through the noise of a dance floor and command a solo style based on sustained tones. The jazz use of this instrument, by men like Floyd Smith and Charlie Christian, shows again how sensitive and expressive a music jazz men can make out of an instrument that concert artists would consider a low in vulgarity. The string bass developed a more independent solo and melodic role, with John Kirby and Israel Crosby leading, and perhaps the greatest influence of all being Ellington's Jimmy Blanton.

The intensification of rhythm took place with the increase of the four-to-the-bar jump beat to the eight-to-the-bar "boogie-woogie" beat and that to the sixteen-to-the-bar bebop beat. The basic beat, of course, was still the 4/4, and these intensifications control the melodic lines, which run counter to the basic beat, entering and leaving on off-beats and accenting the off-beats. All of these rhythmic intensifications could become sheer powerhouse effects. In bebop, however, there is some extraordinary new rhythmic work which can be at the same time genuinely musical. The solos enter and leave at any point within the sixteenth note divisions of the bar. They spin phrases of varying length, seemingly at random and yet satisfyingly controlled. The drums are handled more freely in supporting the solos and producing brilliant drum breaks and surprise clusters of beats. Max Roach, especially, has built up an amazing drum style, employing what seems to be a steady sixteen-note beat on the cymbals as his foundation, and moving about freely in rhythmic patterns with the bass drum and snares.

One of the most important achievements was the solution of the popular ballad problem, out of which came the harmonic exploration and freedom of modern jazz. This was done in many ways. The phrases of the ballad melody could be adorned with little chromatic figures, or broken chords, and modulated into surprising and distant keys. Coleman Hawkins' "Body and Soul" is an example. Its phrases could be rhythmically transformed, turned into riffs, and separated by blues phrases. In this treatment Lester Young is the most extraordinary master. His solos, such as those on "Lady Be Good" with Basie, and on the Billie Holiday records, educated modern tenor sax men in the handling of their instrument and the "blue" treatment of the popular song idiom. There is never any straining for effect, or any obvious harmonic intellectualism, as there often is in Hawkins' work. Young's playing is completely relaxed, and often gives the tune a wholly new musical distinction with the most economical touches, sometimes reducing it to a poignantly repeated note or riff. There is always in his solos a suggestion of the two-voice, antiphonal quality basic to the great jazz solo and a product of the blues. His solos are in the great jazz line, not simply playing about with the melody improvisationally, but creating a new melodic structure of interest and beauty.

Another treatment of the popular tune used it as a bass line, over which a new melody was elaborated as a countervoice, disguising the real theme. Many pre-bebop experiments and bebop performances start with such arrangements based on countervoices to popular tunes, with the original tunes themselves never heard by the listener. Hawkins' "Battle of the Saxes," for example, seems to be "China Boy," Parker's "Ornithology" is "How High the Moon," Gillespie's "Dizzy Atmosphere" and "Dynamo A" are "I Got Rhythm," his (Tempo Jazz Men), "Round About Midnight" adds to the blues a touch of "Louise." Partly out of this kind of handling of the popular tune came a polytonal music, the definite use of two keys at once, of which Gillespie's "I Can't Get Started" and "Things to Come," Parker's "Buzzy" and the end of "Lover Man" are examples. Original themes are invented, serving as opening and closing riffs; themes of great interest and emotional power, and non-diatonic, in that they do not fall completely into any diatonic key. Many of these themes are based, like Ellington's fine "Cotton Tail" theme, on the blues, although so rhyth-mically and melodically free that the original blues exists only in the performer's mind.

In its varied progress, jazz has made a full turn of the wheel, and come back to certain qualities with which it started, but on a new level. A wonderful characteristic of the old jazz had been its feeling of melodic freedom, of harmonic freshness, of speaking its own human and disturbing melodic language. This quality returns in modern jazz.

There are differences between old and new, and important ones. On the one hand, the present language involves and has consciously absorbed the system of diatonic music, the "concert hall" and ballad music, to its immense enrichment; in fact, its possibilities are far richer than the uses that have been so far made of it. On the other hand, the old New Orleans musician made no distinction between his "public" and "private" music. The present day musician suffers from a divided mind, from thinking in terms of two different musical worlds.

There is today, as in the past, the conscious interplay of different musical languages in one work, with fascinating results; the mixture of blues, or of chromatic counter melodies, with popular ballads; the momentary quotation of sweet melodies, often semi-classical fragments, like "Souvenir," "Anitra's Dance," or, as in an unrecorded Parker and Davis performance, an old hymn tune. Sometimes the effect of the mixed languages is atonal, as if key sense were completely absent; sometimes polytonal, with melodies in two distinct keys moving against each other.

A sign of the freedom won by modern jazz, and yet its return to qualities of the old music on a higher level, is the comeback of the blues, bringing, as they did in the past, the most haunting, expressive, personal and collective emotions. But the modern blues are enriched and transformed. The old phrases can be recognized, but with more chromatic twists, richer harmonies, more fluid and varied melodic movement. The change in attitude to the blues has been a steady movement throughout the history of jazz, and a necessary one. An old folk language, no matter how powerful it first was, can become misinterpreted, and over-sweet, in revival. The spirituals, if their true human meaning is not sharply insisted on, can become today an "Uncle Tom" music, of sweet escape. The blues, now that they are taken up by a variety of folklorists, can likewise take on a nostalgic, escapist quality, unless their human symbolism is sharply brought forward.

And so the jazz musicians, particularly the Negro, changed their attitude towards the blues, with their changing conditions and role in society. The blues have taken on more subtle changes of personal mood, and also a more embittered, sardonic character. Examples are Bechet's recent performance of "St. James Infirmary," or the singing of Josh White, the blues playing of Rex Stewart, as in "Solid Rock," Frankie Newton's "The Blues My Baby Gave to Me," the trumpet playing of Joe Guy, the trombone blues of Dickie Wells. Lester Young is saturated in blues idiom, examples being his work in "Lester Leaps In," "Dickie's Dream," "Lester Leaps Again," "Slow Drag," and his blues transformations of popular ballads. Theolonius Monk's "Round About Midnight" is blues in structure and feeling. Blues phrases account for the haunting quality of Gillespie's trumpet figures as in "One Bass Hit" or "Round About Midnight," where he begins by reversing the blues into an upward soaring line, itself suggested by his improvisation on "I Can't Get Started."

Charlie Parker is almost wholly a blues performer, as moving in his own way as Johnny Dodds in the old music. "Billie's Bounce" is perhaps the most extraordinary of his blues solos, with "Cool Blues," "Relaxing at Camarillo's" and "Buzzy" very fine. His use of the blues "break" in "Billie's Bounce" and the Red Norvo "Congo Blues" is a revelation. "The Chase," with Dexter Gorden and Wardell Gray, starts with a haunting blues melody, and then moves into a pattern based on the traditional clarinet solo in "High Society." Certainly the new jazz, like the old, is in great part a national music of the American Negro people, and expressed in it are not only the old experiences of exploitation, but the new ones; the jim-crow army, in the last war; the rising sharpness of the struggle for full citizenship.

What qualities make bebop differ from other modern and experimental jazz, such as that of Ellington, Teddy Wilson, Lester Young, Mary Lou Williams? There is no sharp cleavage. All that can really be said is that bebop has worked out a conscious, sometimes rigid, system from the new elements. Its starting themes are definitely atonal, polytonal or chromatic (the choice of the word depending on the system of analysis one uses). At any rate, these themes seem to start in one key and move immediately into another. Intervals such as seconds, fourths, diminished sevenths, ninths, flattened fifths are consistently used. The soloists consciously work out their performance in terms of these harmonies, both in supporting one another and playing against one another. The sixteenth note bar divisions are consistently used in solos and beat. Performances are based on counter-voices to melodies that are never heard "straight."

Bebop comes close to composed music, in that worked-out performances are highly prized, and repeated many times almost note for note. A fine melodic theme is an achievement, and used as the basis for different performances, as the themes of "The Chase," of "Dizzy Atmosphere" ("Dynamo A"), and "Hothouse." Bebop brings Negro and white musicians working together in closer unity, and matching of ideas, than ever before. To mention "outstanding" names in jazz is always a task to be hesitantly approached. Jazz remains a social music, the product of many musicians and minds. The very commercial, publicity-run nature of the world in which it moves causes some names to rise to prominence, others who made an equal contribution to be ignored. However, just as Parker, Garner, Gillespie, Monk and Dameron can be definitely said to have made a solid contribution, as composers as well as performers, so the pianist Dodo

Mamorosa, the tenor saxophonists Charlie Ventura and Allen Eager may be named among white musicians who have contributed fine technical and musical ideas.

Gillespie, Garner and Ventura exhibit the wit and kidding which are a joyous part of bebop. Parker, who is best in small band music, is the most "blue," introspective and emotionally harrowing. Monk sees always the strange chord, often at the price of an unorganized piece of music. Gillespie, who also invented the term "bebop," organized the most exciting, experimental large band music, aided by composer-arrangers like Les Fuller and John Lewis.

A full appraisal of modern jazz and bebop is a forbidding task, considering the sheer quantity of the records that have been pouring out, under a variety of labels, and the amount of live music that is being heard, some of it more exciting than the records. However, bebop is going through the same trials that afflicted all the other achievements of jazz, including blues, "boogie-woogie," New Orleans music, jump music, Bix styles, "Chicago" style and the rest. There is the main line of creative, genuine and successful music making; there is the experimental wing, in which one often finds a half-successful music, a mechanical use of strange notes and chords simply to be "different"; there is the commercialization, the uncritical publicizing of bad and good, mostly bad, together, the taking over of the new achievement for innumerable imitations that only serve to bring bewilderment to listeners.

The modern experimental jazz, a term better than bebop for the new jazz music heard today, is a bundle of contradictions. It works with the basic method of folk art, improvisation, but demands the utmost harmonic education and sensitivity from the improvisors. It advances boldly into composition, but because of the conditions under which it must work out its ideas, it often sounds like a magnificent opening to a musical work not followed by any development. It brings together Negro and white musicians in a tighter unity and musical collaboration than ever before in the history of jazz. But it also has aspects of faddism. It dabbles with the superficial philosophical lingo of existentialism, and with unique styles of speech and dress, as if it were a cult. It attracts many of the most thoughtful musicians in jazz, and also suffers from nerve-strain, and the drink and narcotic by-products of the insecurity of jazz life. It produces genial records like "A Night in Tunisia," "Congo Blues," and "Dizzy Atmosphere," and also haunting records like "The Chase," or Parker's sick, nerve-wracked "Lover Man," made when he was at the point of collapse. It is a music full of melody, although this melody, made up of the blues or of countervoices to popular tunes, takes keen listening to follow its strange twists and turns. Yet it also produces a wholly unmelodic music, which in its mechanical use of "new" chords, modulations and instrumental timbres only sounds like the less inspired music created by modern European composers. Some of it belongs with the most lasting and beautiful music of jazz. Some of it is merely light and witty entertainment, and only gets by with its audiences because they are not familiar with the better "classical" composed music exploiting similar harmonies and timbres. Most of Stan Kenton's music seems to this writer to consist of this kind of entertainment. But the presence and popularity even of this music has its commentary to make on the idiocy of our present division between the "classical" and "popular" worlds of music. For the followers of this "popular" music are actually enjoying a harmonic, rhythmic and instrumental idiom that still seems "advanced" and hard to take to many patrons of the concert halls.

Bebop and modern jazz have by no means settled the problems of jazz. In fact, they raise the contradictions inherent in jazz from its beginnings, to their highest level. These contradictions within a music are directly a product of the contradictions in our social life, predominantly rising out of the place of the Negro people in American life.

By this I do not mean that jazz is exclusively a music of the Negro people, or a problem of the Negro people. I mean that the culture of an entire people, like its democracy, cannot be understood or put on a healthy footing without solving the problem of the culture, and political freedom, of the minority peoples who together make up its great majority. The largest and most exploited minority is the Negro people. I have already taken up, in the first chapter, some of the reasons for the predominance of the Negro people in jazz. This was not due to any physical characteristics, "African" or otherwise. The Negro people in America have a tradition of achievement and struggle which goes all the way back to Africa, but have no longer a direct line of physical ancestry to Africa. They are thoroughly mixed in heritage, as are all of us. The Negro born in a Northern city environment is as likely to find the blues and spirituals strange to him, or to be as clumsy on a dance floor, as his white fellow citizen. On the other hand white city dwellers can discover and master rhythm, love and use the blues, when they feel the living need for these forms of art and life. The Negro and white have exactly the same potentialities either for jazz or for conducting a Schubert symphony.

The predominance of the Negro people in jazz is due to social and cultural reasons; the need of the Negro communities to make their own entertainment, the place that song and dance held in the life of Negro children, the special social and emotional content that entered the music created by the Negro people. What they had to say could not be directly expressed otherwise except in real and sharp struggle, such as accompanied the development of jazz. There is a direct line of development from the old jazz to the new, a line of change, not of static preservation of old qualities. Modern jazz is a human and social musical expression not, as the "purists" would have it, a commercial conspiracy. The old jazz was a protest against the narrowness of semi-feudal, Southern life, in the years before the first world war, using the idioms and forms given it by semi-feudal life. Modern jazz is a protest against monopoly control of music and the commodity-like exploitation of the musicians, a protest using the idioms and forms given it by commercial music.

In modern times the Negro musician has led the jazz field for new added reasons. What operates heavily now is the jim-crow and discrimination directed against the Negro in the classical music field, a powerful factor now that the Negro musician has slowly won his battle to include in his music, change or reject if he wishes, all the developments in science, method and technique of world music. The musical education of the Negro people is drastically low, far lower than that, bad as it is, given to white children. The luxury of attending a music school or conservatory is difficult for the Negro, due to his being kept in the lowest paid jobs. Jim-crow pervades all the better paying jobs and professions. Jim-crow pervades music, on radio, in Hollywood, in opera and symphony. It is enlightening to anyone who thinks that discrimination or prejudice come from poor "education," to discover that discrimination multiplies geometrically as we go up the social ladder. Symphony orchestras are far behind jazz bands in recognizing Negro talent. A conductor of the outstanding ability of Dean Dixon cannot get a job conducting. Singers of the calibre of Marian Anderson, Roland Hayes, Paul Robeson, Carol Brice, Dorothy Maynor, never get a nod from the Metropolitan opera, which has employed even second-rate and third-rate singers for their connections and Hollywood glamour. In movies, on radio, on Broadway, the Negro is jim-crowed, allowed to work, if at all, as a special kind of entertainer, never permitted to fill a role simply because he is best able to fill it. The major symphony orchestras hire no Negro performers, well-equipped as some of them are. The Negro people have no music schools, music theatre, musical organizations of their own, through which they can take part in the broad musical life possible in our times.

Thus the creative imagination of the Negro musician has been poured largely into the narrow frame of dance and light entertainment music, often stretching the boundaries of this form to the very limit. The results have benefited American song and dance music by immeasurably raising its musical quality and emotional content. They have permitted great fortunes to be earned, less often by the creative musician than by the merchandiser able to cash in on the latest "novelty" he could make out of some innovation by a Negro musician. It is because so much talent and genius have been poured into jazz music, old and new, that this music has its present quality.

But modern jazz, for this very reason, is not a completely satisfactory music. There is too great a disparity between the musical ideas, the inventiveness applied to them, the emotions demanding expression, and the narrow forms. Some modern jazz sounds overweighted harmonically and overelaborate in instrumental texture, without the melodic line and structure to carry the ideas forward. The reason is that there is a horizontal as well as vertical character to music, and the two must be proportionate. Some musical problems, like those facing a painter and writer, require space to work themselves out. A Michelangelo couldn't put his Sistine Chapel conceptions on a postcard; a Tolstoi couldn't put the emotions of "Anna Karenina" into a magazine short-short; a Beethoven couldn't put the emotions of the "Appassionata" into a scherzo.

Jazz has reached a kind of impasse, a peak beyond which it can go no further within the forms in which it exists today. There may be slight innovations, such as the use of new rhythms, new instruments, larger orchestras. But these are minor changes. Jazz, for its next step forward, calls for a change as radical and sweeping as that which took place when it moved up the Mississippi River. It is knocking at the door of musical composition, in more ambitious forms, and must enter.

This thought may bring violent protest from those who cannot see anything new, or who say that composed music is classical music, "for whites only" (disguising this jim-crow by all kinds of praise for the wonderful

Negro "folk," and all kinds of epithets directed against the "degenerate" practise of composing music); jazz is pure improvisation, and never the twain shall meet. It may bring serious questions from those who prize the improvisational character of jazz, and feel that it thus adds something unique to our musical culture which should not be taken away.

However, we have seen that there is no absolute division between improvised and composed music. They are different, but not hermetically sealed from one another. The difference is not between two different worlds of music, but between two different uses of music. Improvisation is an amateur, folk and peoples' way of making music, immensely important for its genuine entertainment, its development of fresh musical ideas, its making music a part of personal and social life. Larger forms of music demand composition, the working out of music to embody more complex problems of human conflict and emotion, more subtle portrayals of the processes of human thought. Composed music does not negate improvised. Modern civilization requires the musical expression to be found in the more ambitious forms and structures, just as it needs the amateur spirit, the participation in music of large masses of people, the influx of new language materials that can only come from widespread folk and musical improvisation. The two can be of the greatest musical assistance. It is when the composed forms are most accessible to people, and advance most freely, that improvisation also advances and spreads enormously. Similarly, we can say that if we had a nation-wide theatre, a living stage in every sizeable community, not only would the writing of fine plays be multiplied but the progress of amateur and semi-professional dramatic life among the people would advance equally. Modern jazz is a living music, but even more, has within it a new music, clamoring to be born.

The problem of the next step forward, however, is a social as well as a musical problem. The Negro people have not been content to be treated as second-class citizens, discriminated against, made the butt of insult. They have fought for equality in pay, equal opportunities for jobs, votes and education with all other American people. This struggle, carried on in the political and economic fields, has also been carried on in music. It is reflected in the kind of advances that took place in jazz during the 'thirties and 'forties. It is also reflected in the increasing struggle of Negro people for a musical education and a foothold in the concert and opera world.

The next step calls for a democratic change in our entire musical culture. It involves the breakdown of the last vestiges of snobbery towards folk, amateur and popular art production; the broadening of the classical musical picture, so that musical education is more widespread, providing more opportunities for American composers to reach American audiences, and a healthier spirit in composed music; the breakdown of the barriers which prevent the minority peoples, and especially the Negro people, from taking an active part in musical production on every level, from the most immediately popular forms of art to the most advanced and ambitious structures. In other words the next step for jazz is bound up with the breakdown of discrimination wherever it is found in our social and cultural life.

RECORD ILLUSTRATIONS—CHAPTER SIX

ELLINGTON

East St. Louis Toodle-oo, The Mooche, Mood Indigo, Ring Dem Bells, Stompy Jones, Delta Serenade, Dusk, Warm Valley (in Victor Album P-138) East St. Louis Toodle-oo, Birmingham Breakdown, Rocking in Rhythm, Black and Tan Fantasy, The Mooche, Mood Indigo, Wall St. Wail (in Brunswick Album B-1000) Black and Tan Fantasy, Creole Love Call (Victor 24861) Echoes of Harlem (Columbia 36283) Bragging in Brass (Columbia 36276) Sophisticated Lady, Stormy Weather (Columbia 35556) Across the Track (Victor 27235) Cotton Tail (Victor 26610) Do Nothing Till You Hear From Me (Concerto for Cootie) (Victor 20-1547) Jack the Bear (Victor 36536) A Portait of Bert Williams (Victor 26644) Take the A Train (Victor 27380) That's the Blues, Old Man (Hodges) (Victor 20-2542)

BASIE

Dogging Around (Decca 18125) One O'Clock Jump (Decca 25056) How Long How Long Blues (piano and rhythm section) (Decca 2355)

DEVELOPMENT OF THE KANSAS CITY RIFF AND JUMP

Mary Lou Williams—Harmony Blues, Baby Dear (Decca 18122)

Oran "Hot Lips" Page and Band—South, Lafayette (Decca 18122)

Kansas City Seven—Destination K.C. (Keynote 1303)

Benny Goodman and his Sextet—Air Mail Special (Columbia 36720)

Charlie Christian—In the Hall of the Mountain King (Vox Album 302)

"Dizzy" Gillespie—Blue'n Boogie (Musicraft 486)

Chu Berry—Maelstrom (Columbia 37571)

Gillespie—Good Bait (Manor 1042)

Gillespie—Emmanon, Things to Come (Musicraft 447)

Errol Garner—Loose Nut (Dial 1095)

TRANSFORMATION OF THE POPULAR BALLAD AND BEBOP

Billie Holiday—I Wished On the Moon (Columbia 36205)

Bunny Berigan—I Can't Get Started (Victor 20-1500)

Gillespie—I Can't Get Started (Manor 1042)

Lester Young Trio—I Can't Get Started, Tea for Two, Body and Soul, Indiana (Philo 1000, 1001)

Hall-Wilson Quartet—Where or When (Commodore 570)

Lester Young Quartet—Sometimes I'm Happy (Keynote 604)

Goodman and his Sextet—As Long as I Live (Columbia 36723)

"Red" Norvo and Sextet—Hallelujah, Get Happy (Comet 6, 7)

Art Tatum—Sweet Lorraine, Get Happy (Decca 25200)

Coleman Hawkins—Bean Stalking ("Idaho")—(Asch 3551)

Kansas City Seven—After Theatre Jump ("Dardanella")

Cozy Cole's All Stars—Curry in a Hurry ("Sweet Georgia Brown") (Keynote 1305)

Jazz at the Philharmonic—Vol. 1 How High The Moon (Stinson 453)

Charlie Parker Septet—Bird Lore (Dial 1006) or Ornithology (Dial 1102) ("How High the Moon")

Charlie Parker Septet—A Night in Tunisia (Dial 1002) ("O Katherina"? "Caravan"?)

"Dizzy" Gillespie—Dizzy Atmosphere (Musicraft 488) and Tempo Jazz Men (with Gillespie)—Dynamo A (Dial 1001) ("I've Got Rhythm")

Charlie Parker—Lover Man (Dial 1007)

· "Dizzy" Gillespie, with Sarah Vaughan—Lover Man (Musicraft 354)

"Dizzy" Gillespie—Hothouse (Musicraft 486) ("What is This Thing Called Love")

DEVELOPMENT OF THE BLUES AND BEBOP

Mel Powell and Orchestra—Mood at Twilight (Commodore 544)

Hawkins, Young and Clayton—Slow Drag (Clef 103)—in Jazz at the Philharmonic, Vol. 6)

Kansas City Seven—Lester Leaps Again (Keynote 1302)

"Red" Norvo and Sextet—Congo Blues, "Slam Slam" Blues (Comet 7, 6)

Theolonius Monk Quintet—Round About Midnight (Musicraft 543)

Errol Garner—Blues Garni (Dial 1093)

Jazz at the Philharmonic—The Blues (Vol 4, Disc 504)

Tempo Jazz Men—Round About Midnight (Dial 1001)

Charlie Parker's Reeboppers—Billie's Bounce (Savoy 573)

Charlie Parker All Stars—Relaxin' at Camarillo (Dial 1012)

Cool Blues, Blowtop Blues (Dial 1054)

Dexter Gordon and Wardell Gray—The Chase (Dial 1017)

Lucky Thompson and his Lucky Seven—Boppin' the Blues (Victor 20-2504)

Charlie Parker Quintet—Buzzy (Savoy 652)

While Ellington is well represented on available records, there are a great many outstanding performances out of print, including some of as recent vintage as Victor's "Ko Ko," "Conga Brava," and "Mobile Bay" (Rex Stewart). Victor also has in its files some of the fine early performances, such as "Jubilee Stomp," "Got Everything

But You," "Saratoga Swing," "Black Beauty." Columbia should restore such old classics as "Ducky Wucky," "Rocky Mountain Blues," "Boy Meets Horn," and a healthy selection of the fine small group records made under the name of Bigard, Williams, Greer and Hodges, such as "Caravan," "Delta Mood," "Minuet in Blues," "Saturday Night Function," "Echoes of Harlem," "Dooji Wooji."

At least twenty out-of-print Basie sides should be made available, from the Decca and Columbia files, including "Swinging the Blues," both "Lady Be Good" performances, "Taxi War Dance," "Twelfth St. Rag," "Jump for Me," "Topsy," "Lester Leaps In," "Dickie's Dream," "Sent For You Yesterday." A selection of the Teddy Wilson small group recordings, and the Holiday-Young collaborations, such as "Back in Your Own Back Yard" and "The Man I Love" would also be worth having about.

The credit for recording the modern experimental jazz goes mainly to the small record companies, generally guided by enthusiasts who are willing to follow in the tracks of the growing music itself, instead of setting up standard routines for the musicians to fit. Small companies too, of course, can produce bad jazz. The records listed above, however, all contain, in this writer's opinion, music of lasting quality, and varied enough in mood and personnel to show the wide range of modern jazz.

CHAPTER SEVEN

THE FUTURE OF JAZZ

Any theories regarding the relation of jazz to musical composition must start by rejecting the major part of what has passed up to now for composed jazz.

To approach the problem correctly, we must remember that jazz is a great and powerful music in its own right, within the forms of song and dance that it has made its own. Any composed music using jazz must have at least equal power. Some qualities will necessarily be lost, such as the unpredictable flights of imagination, the contagious relationship between a musical creator and a responsive audience, in an improvised performance. The composed music will have to make up for this lack in other ways.

The greater amount of jazz tone poems, jazz concertos, symphonic jazz and jazz operas, however, while
offered as an "improvement" on jazz, do not come anywhere near the musical taste, inventiveness, and beauty
of jazz itself. In fact the greater part of serious composed
music in America, whether or not it has touches of jazz,
does not come anywhere near jazz for musical vitality
and emotional power. It is little wonder that most people
who love jazz look upon attempts at jazz composition as
compounded of pretentiousness, publicity-seeking novelty, and sheer ignorance of any but the most superficial
characteristics of jazz music. Most attempts at composed
jazz have been exactly of this nature.

The problem is not to be solved only by a new
method, or by a new approach to the writing of music.
New musical forms are not invented in books. They come
about through new methods of presenting music to
people. And so, while some approaches can be sketched
out here, their success depends upon a re-orientation of
much of our musical culture; the opening of new avenues through which composer, performer and audience
can come together. American music, whether jazz or
concert-hall, has long been crying for such an orientation.

Any program for the use of jazz in musical composition must not negate or displace the amateur, folk and
improvisational spirit in jazz and American music. However, jazz has long since stopped being exclusively a folk
art, although it uses folk material lavishly. The current

revival of New Orleans jazz does not restore a folk art to America. It brings back a beautiful music no longer creative because its social environment no longer exists. Although this music originally grew through improvisation, it is no longer performed with any real amount of improvisation, but follows closely fixed, remembered patterns. If the great qualities of New Orleans music are to be revived, they must get a new life on the basis of new social conditions, which will enable the music again to become living, experimental and changing. This means that the music itself will be different.

The blues, sung and performed on whatever instruments people find at hand, are still a potent American folk music. Their continuation rests, however, not on what happens to jazz but on what happens to the American people, on how much they are permitted to create their own music, to invent and inspire their own entertainment. It is important to continue the folk art of America, which is rapidly retreating under the impact of packaged and manufactured synthetic culture. But if the blues are given a new lease on life, they will change, just as the blues themselves rose out of and alongside the spirituals. What new folk music will come is as unpredictable as what new experiences people will encounter, and what words and music they will invent to describe them.

The problem of jazz composition is a pressing one because jazz itself has raised this question. And the question was raised long before jazz performers were talking about ninth chords and critics were discussing Duke Ellington in learned musical terms; long before Paul Whiteman introduced the "Rhapsody in Blue" to a concert audience and George Gershwin began thinking of writing an "opera." Jazz composition is practically as old as jazz itself. It rose in New Orleans. Scott Joplin, one of the most celebrated figures in early jazz, was known as a composer of piano rags, and wrote an operetta dealing with Negro history and using rag music. Ferdinand Morton was a composer. His assertion that he "invented jazz" is not literally true, but expresses his justified resentment at being considered a clown or purveyor of light entertainment, his demand to be recognized as a musical creator. His piano rags, especially those in his Library of Congress records, issued by Circle, stand up as musical compositions; some of them elaborate ones, like the musical depiction of a New Orleans funeral, also recorded in condensed form on a band record called "Oh Didn't He Ramble." If we compare the several existing records of "The Pearls," both piano and band, we will find much the same fixed musical conception in all of them.

And so, in the very birth of jazz, the process started, unpretentiously and generally with higher quality, that has now reached a climax with jazz concertos and tone poems galore, Stan Kenton and others producing works with titles like "Fugue for Percussion," jazz arrangers studying Stravinsky, Schoenberg and the Schillinger system. The latter is most popular, for, perhaps unintended by its creator, it teaches how seemingly new melodies can be made out of old ones by stretching or contracting the intervals and rhythms according to mathematical principles; a perfect system for producing the mock-human music demanded by tin-pan-alley. The question today is no longer whether jazz is to be composed, but whether its composition is to be put on a musically sincere and productive track.

And this is a problem of American composed music as well as of jazz. American composition is calling for the qualities that jazz can give. It needs a language, fresh, flexible and communicative, with recognizable human images so that it can make contact with its listeners. Nothing is more indicative of the unsolved problem of idiom than the fact that American composers go to Stravinsky, Schoenberg, medieval music, Chinese music, Balinese music and everywhere else for ideas except to the musical language which exists under their noses. This is the contradiction of present-day American music. The jazz men who want to expand their art, to take on new emotional and structural problems, and who have the richest material at their fingertips, are not sure of where to turn, of what lessons to study. The composer who has mastered the know-how, who has absorbed the long traditions of music, is at a loss for a language.

The attempts made up to now to compose music using jazz are valuable mainly as examples of what not to do. The most prominent of such composers was George Gershwin. Gershwin was one of the great creative talents, a genius or near genius, of American popular music. And the word popular is used not as a limiting expression, but only to describe the circle in which he moved.

He was a jazz figure, although he lacked many of the qualities of hot jazz. His songs were made possible by jazz. "It Ain't Necessarily So" and "I Got Plenty of Nothin' " are jazz-doctored spirituals; "Summertime" and "The Man I Love" are unthinkable without the blues; "I Got Rhythm," "Swanee," "Lady Be Good," "Embraceable You," are born of rag music. These songs, fashioned out of the collective body of jazz, still have his own unique personality and melodic invention, and were in turn welcomed by jazz. Yet as songs they have deficiencies, which can be seen by measuring Gershwin alongside of the "classical" songwriting genius, Franz Schubert.

Schubert was by no means "highbrow." Writing in the early 1800's, he used themes and styles from Austrian folk songs, the rhythms and melodic curves of the popular marches, waltzes, and *landler*, the precursor of the waltz. His music in fact was severely taken to task by the more narrowminded critics of the time because it seemed to them to be too popular, or "vulgar" in idiom. But in handling this idiom, he studied the most advanced and best masters of musical composition of his time, and the immediate past, such as Haydn, Mozart and Beethoven.

This does not mean that he used what he learned from them to put his melodic ideas into fancy dress, which has come to be the modern arranger's idea of using classical music. He learned rather how to put his ideas into the most succinct, economical and powerful form, how to squeeze the water out of his compositions. He learned his craft thoroughly, and it is always when a musician's knowledge is too little rather than too much that he falls into bombast and platitudes.

He set his songs to poems that, while easy to understand, were genuinely poetic and meaningful; some of them by Shakespeare, Goethe, and Heine. His songs took different forms suggested by the emotions and structure of the poems. His piano accompaniments were as inventive as the vocal lines.

By all these standards Gershwin fell short. Because of the environment in which he worked, he never mastered a workable musical craft. His tunes were not allowed to deviate in form, bar pattern, stanza, climax, from the standard sheet-music straight jacket. The words were the meaningless variations on the inane themes of Broadway lyric writing, in his case somewhat sharpened in rhyme scheme and wit, but still drastically limited in human content. His harmonization was based on a few cliches, and the orchestration, as well as much of the harmonization, was often provided by somebody else, according to the Broadway-Hollywood ultra-specialization, so destructive to quality, by which one man writes a melody, another harmonizes it, a third orchestrates it. The scope of the Broadway musical show for which he wrote was similarly narrow and uninspiring, lacking good sense and acceptable human characterization. Gershwin's songs are a tragic example of a partially successful art, of a fine talent which never found a mature and effective means of expression.

Realizing this lack and trying to acquire better musical forms and tools, Gershwin took a step forward which landed him in the overblown tradition of nineteenth century opera, overture, rhapsody and concerto. It is easy to see why this music should have seemed to him to be the summit of the "classical" art, for it permeated the concert world of his as of our own times. But the musical tools he got from this study were already outworn.

There is music of real quality in the "Rhapsody in Blue," "Concerto in F," "An American in Paris." They have dancing melodies of tender and sprightly feeling, rhythms which as in real jazz laugh at bar lines, a touch of the jazz instrument. These are mixed with meaningless elements; modulations used simply to vary the tonality, repetitions brought in simply to conform to "classical" structure. Anyone who knows real jazz becomes painfully aware of the absence in these works of the wonderful qualities jazz could have added, qualities for which it cries out; the powerful rock of a hot jazz rhythm section, the clean instrumentation of clarinet, trumpet, trombone and sax, economically used; blues intonations, and free jazz polyphony. Yet because there is a thread of real music in these works, they have been exciting to hear, with a live, songful idiom at their heart which raises them far above more perfectly worked out but barren works coming from the conservatories.

The trouble is the same with "Of Thee I Sing" and "Porgy and Bess." The satiric honesty of the first show made it a work of quality. Yet to supply the musical and structural ideas for this new stage form, Gershwin fell back on the weak props of Gilbert and Sullivan. "Porgy and Bess" was written as an attempt to portray the Negro people with sympathy, but had little realism and under-standing. The central factor in an understanding of the real life of the Negro people of the South, their relation to white people and a white economy, was little touched on, and so his "Catfish Row" took on the aspect of a sen-timental fairy tale, a childishness, a slumming expedition. The music likewise sentimentalized the melodic germs it took from spirituals and jazz, dressing them up in a pseudo-symphonic fabric.

These works had an impact for good, since the live human and musical elements they contained exposed the idiocy of the average Broadway musical show. They re-affirmed the truth that commercial producers will never recognize, that the public prefers art of human quality to trash. Good music and good sense, given an equal chance to reach the public, will always drive out the bad.

The Gershwin compositions proved that the jazz idiom had real vitality as part of a concert piece, for all its dilution. The Gershwin shows raised the level of the Broadway musical, so that the new plots were tempered with some sense. But nobody took the next step of clearing up Gershwin's contradictions, and his weaknesses were as much repeated as his strong points. Symphonic jazz and jazz concertos of the past years have all the cliches, without the freshness, of the Gershwin pieces. The Broadway musicals, even the touted Rodgers-Hammerstein series, call themselves operas and lift some practises out of Puccini, but are less exciting and more pretentious than the Gershwin efforts.

Ellington's ambitious jazz compositions, such as "Black, Brown and Beige" and "Liberia Suite," are a step above Gershwin's in that they have more real jazz qualities. They are live and exciting in melody, rhythm and instrumental timbre. But they also suffer from incomplete theory and knowledge. The good parts, and they are many, have quality in the sense that the best of Ellington's dance pieces have quality. But the qualities that made Ellington's shorter works completely successful are inadequate for so ambitious a step forward in psychological, historical and dramatic content. The music Ellington composes to knit the dance and song sections of these works together are often simple, repeated rhythmic patterns with dissonant chords, less moving than his dance music instead of more. He has not evolved enough of a new craft to match his new and exciting ideas. These works, however, are transitional ones. Their very production was made possible by a personal struggle against the circumscribed routine in which a band leader must move. Our musical life does not make it economically possible for so phenomenal a band as Ellington built up to be permanently held together, nor does it make it economically possible for Ellington to spend the time necessary to work out a music that could be so valuable an addition to our culture.

Out of Ellington's work have likewise come a number of efforts at composing music for jazz band, by such arrangers as Eddie Sauter and Pete Rugulo, the latter working out most of Kenton's pieces. But these works add nothing to what Ellington has done, and are on a lower musical level, chiefly in exactly that department in which jazz should be strong, its instrumental sound. The solo sections are in the jazz tradition, but the merged sounds are muddy, lacking in the finesse of combined harmony and timbre that the Duke displays in all of his work.

If the attempts of jazz men to compose music are weak, the attempts of learned composers to write using jazz are equally weak, but for different reasons. Examples are Igor Stravinsky's "Ragtime" and parts of his "Histoire du Soldat"; Darius Milhaud's ballet "La Création du Monde"; Maurice Ravel's two piano concertos and violin sonata; Arthur Honegger's concertino for piano and sections of his cantata "Joan of Arc"; Ernst Krenek's opera

"Johnny Spielt Auf"; Kurt Weil's light operas, from "Three-penny Opera" to "Street Scene"; the work of some Americans such as Aaron Copland and Marc Blitzstein.

Most of these works were composed in the experimental 'twenties, or in a style that was then given shape. The choice of idiom was suggested by the revulsion against the industrial world, and the disillusionment that followed the First World War. The arts took flight from all sentimentalities, and also from all forthright, positive emotions. They sought influences in the medieval, in the Asiatic, in the folk, any place but the mainstream of European culture. Such a movement in the arts had been germinating ever since the 1890's, with Gauguin's brilliant paintings of the South Seas; Debussy's experiment with folk, Asiatic and non-diatonic musical scale; Satie's mocking piano pieces, apparently music-hall in idiom but polished in every note; Picasso's painting inspired by African sculpture; Stravinsky's mechanistic handling of melodic and rhythmic germs taken from folk lore. These tendencies reached a climax in the 'twenties.

Jazz was taken up as another exotic and primitivistic idiom. Needless to say its true qualities, its wealth of folk melody, its many strong and solid forms, its polyphonic subtlety, its warmth, tenderness and humor, were ignored. For one reason, they were not known. For another, the tendency, loudly proclaimed as "anti-bourgeois," was also against any real appreciation of the common people and their art. The intellectual really turned to his private misconception of the common man, in the mood of one who, seemingly sick of civilization, decides to live among "savages."

Much of this music was quite beautiful. The composers who created it were knowing and finished craftsmen, with a fine command of harmony and orchestral sound, and an ability to create a pleasing musical texture about idioms of any description from jazz to Spanish music, Hungarian, Indian, Balinese, satiric distortions of Viennese Waltzes and Mendelssohn's Wedding March, and anything else they fancied. Typical is the Ravel piano concerto, with hints of ragtime in its opening movement, a slow movement in three-quarter time reminding one of Satie, with a shimmering, impressionist accompaniment, and a last movement with brass glissandos and loud drum beats seemingly meant to depict "Le Jazz Hot." His Piano Concerto for the Left Hand offers as jazz mechanistic, Stravinskian rhythms really foreign to jazz. Milhaud's "La Création du Monde," using lush saxophone timbres, is a little more sensuous. Stravinsky's few measures of ragtime in his "Histoire du Soldat," which rubs elbows with a tango, waltz and march, are amazing in the economy with which the composer catches the feeling of a jazz band, although one seen through a glass darkly. The work has elements which make it a textbook in instrumental timbre and musical pessimism, but lacks the humanity of jazz.

The German works such as Weil's and Krenek's are different from the French in their approach to jazz but even poorer. There is no search for the exotic, the "primitive," the pseudo folk. Rather jazz is accepted as a "bourgeois" music, and the tawdriness of the torch song, the blaring insensitivity of the imitation ragtime, are exaggerated with expressionistic irony. The feeling is that of dancing on a grave, like the caricatures drawn by George Grosz.

The Americans, strangely enough, use jazz in somewhat the same manner as the Europeans. Copland, in his Jazz Piano concerto, "Music for the Theatre" and "El Salon Mexico," is close to Stravinsky and the French; Blitzstein, in his "The Cradle Will Rock," close to the German. It may seem queer to people of other countries who have come to know and love jazz that talented American composers should not know their own folk music, but such ignorance is typical of our cultural life. The great research into jazz was carried on not by musicians or musicologists but by amateurs who loved the music, and hardly regarded themselves in any other respect as students of music. It was natural for serious composers, brought up with academic training, to regard jazz as nothing but vulgarism. Then, when they went abroad or were influenced by the harmony, the anti-academicism, the new and exciting musical systems that came from abroad, they "rediscovered" jazz as the European experimenter saw it.

In the blaring brass and thumping drums of the Copland piano concerto there is no hint of the real beauty of a trumpet solo by Joe Smith, or the subtle weaving of rhythmic patterns by a Baby Dodds or Cozy Cole. His piano writing hints at simple percussive ragtime or torch-song blues, without approaching the charm of a Morton piano, the rhythmic brilliance of a Hines, the rich sonorities and fine registration of a Yancey. Still the music well expresses Copland's own feelings, his lament and violent agitation. Within its limits it is a successful work, its instrumental writing economical, its harmonies interesting. It has only superficial resemblance, however, to jazz.

Marc Blitzstein, in his "The Cradle Will Rock," does not go deeply into jazz. What he has drawn upon mostly is the torch-song imitation of the blues, the ragtime syncopation, the crooner saccharinity, the twang of a Hawaiian guitar. He handles these elements with sharp humor and musical invention. The torch-song idiom portrays movingly the pathos of the Moll, in "The Nickel Under Your Foot"; the crooner lingo becomes a fine satiric tool, as in the "Honolulu" song; jump music also becomes satire, as in the "Freedom of the Press" and the Minister scene. These are accomplishments which justify this work being called the best Broadway musical show, the first great step forward after Gershwin, and one of the best operas produced in America from the standpoint of the unity of words and music, and the high level of both. But the comparative weaknesses of the music, its thin positive emotions as compared to the finesse of its pathos and satire, are exactly the weaknesses of Blitz-stein's approach to jazz. It is this positive emotion which the great jazz has and the commercial dilutions lack; real tenderness, protest, exuberant joy in life, the assertion of the power of human beings to triumph over the conditions that would grind them down.

The very fact that Blitzstein did so much with so small a range of musical idiom shows what can be done with jazz in the larger musical forms. "The Cradle Will Rock" opens up new paths, and necessary ones for jazz. It created a popular dramatic and song art honest in words, true and clear in human images, related to the problems people met in their daily lives. It had both anger and laughter, free of the self-pity, sentimentality and sense of defeat that usually attends the false, "slice-of-life" kind of realism, and makes audiences cry for "escape." It combined a completely singable musical line with a full composer's craft knowledge. The songs could have been popular hits, had not the undercover censorship of the music distribution industry given them the brush-off. At the same time these songs had profile, varied structure, a matching of vocal line with fine piano and instrumental texture, sensitive harmonization, freedom from padding. The music proved the truth that a composer's craft is best shown when the audience is unconscious of its existence, and only knows that the music itself lives.

This work and a handful of others, such as Earl

Robinson's "Ballad for Americans" and "The Lonesome Train," the first written with John La Touche and the second with Millard Lampell, show how much new quality popular and folk music, whether jazz, spirituals, blues or cowboy song, can take on when the form, the words, the relation to life and people's needs, give the composer some elbow room. They hint at what could be accomplished by a music drama created by Negro composers, performers, poets and playwrights, with full freedom to explore the realities of life and American history. There were times when Broadway did feel the need to use some living jazz, and even the work of Negro musicians, as in the "Shuffle Along," "Gold Digger" and "Running Wild" shows, and the more recent "Beggar's Holiday" with music by Ellington. But these shows were, of necessity, a compromise with the standardized manner of Broadway entertainment. The lyric writers and composers had little elbow room, little real inspiration to expand their musical ideas. The shows as a whole had to obey the prevalent snob conception of how the Negro must appear on a stage. Such works, in their final form, were a mockery of what a true national music and dramatic art could be.

Jazz can be a fit idiom for a great music, but this does not mean that the folk song or jazz writer can rush brashly into the job of creating an opera, symphony or concerto. Music, like every other art, requires accumulated knowledge and practised craftsmanship. In New

Orleans, where performers reached great heights with limited study, the lack was made up for by the traditions handed down from one performer to another, and the wealth of forms that rose out of the integration of music with the community life. But this music, like all of the great folk cultures, was limited.

The larger musical forms, like opera, cantata, concerto and symphony, rose out of the need to handle more profound and subtle problems of emotional conflict, human characterization and drama. These forms do not replace the forms of dance and song, any more than the invention of the automobile replaces the need for walking. The larger forms serve new purposes, and they interrelate most tightly with song and dance. It was from song and dance that great composers of the past got the language, the union of musical patterns with human images, that they used in their symphonic and operatic works.

Today, great numbers of the Negro people are struggling for a foothold in the concert world, as singers, instrumental performers, composers. They are kept out of this world not only by outright discrimination, but by the roundabout discrimination which praises their "folk art," and asks that they stay within its limits. The Negro people rightly feel, however, that they are not only entitled to share in all the cultural forms and tools that the progress of life has brought into being, but need them for their own cultural progress. In these new and broader

forms all the qualities of the older art can return, necessarily transformed but still powerful. And when musical
composition is thus free to move into many different
channels, improvisation will again return in full force to
our song and dance forms. Improvisation will become
what it should be; a means for musical enjoyment, as
during the last war when groups of soldiers would gather
about anyone who had a guitar, fiddle or harmonica, and
the members of every military band would relax in a
jam session. It can be a means through which new popular languages will slowly form, through which the

musical performer can give his work a creative and personal character, through which the composer can work out new ideas. It is worth remembering that the eighteenth century, when improvisation was so prolific, was also a great century for composition, with both often carried on by the same men.

During the past century, there was a great revival of folk music, and of composition based on it, in such countries as Bohemia, Poland, Italy, Russia, the Scandinavian countries, and others, where some musicians resented the snobbish importation of a seemingly "advanced" culture to the detriment of the cultural life that had to be built at home. Out of such "national" movements came an appreciation of the wealth of folk music, but also a host of showy and shallow rhapsodies, fantasies and concert pieces based on folk songs, adding little or nothing to the folk music itself. The weakness of much of this music was due to the fact that the national movements themselves, which the art reflected, did not base themselves on the democratic needs and progress of all the people. The music became, like the national movements themselves, wrapped up in sentimental folksiness and longing for the "good old past," behind which the leaders of the one country only sought to duplicate at home the exploiting practises which they resented in the "advanced" countries. Instead of looking at a national culture, like national freedom, as a goal to which all peoples could move together, in friendly collaboration, the "national" culture was upheld in opposition to any tools for progress that could be gathered elsewhere, with the result that the homegrown culture took on the same shoddy quality as the worst importation.

In our own country bitter experience has taught us that national freedom is inseparable from the democratic struggle, and the future of one people is wrapped up with the future of all. At the same time composers have provided us with a wealth of new material in the use of folk material for musical composition. Some of these composers are Claude Debussy, Leo Janacek, Jan Sibelius, Ralph Vaughan Williams, Bela Bartok, Serge Prokofiev, Dmitri Shostakovich, Manuel De Falla, Charles Ives. The lessons taught by these composers are wrapped up in their works, and are not to be lifted out mechanically. And some of these composers, struggling for art to fit the needs of their own generation, show limitations in regard to the needs of our own times. But in general they worked along the lines of exploring the new harmonic implications of folk melody; restoring polyphonic music, based on melodic line, as against an over lush use of harmonic color; using new instrumental combinations, clean and fresh in texture and often based on folk instrumental timbres; combining the best of the symphonic and operatic tradition with the new traditions of folk music, so that the psychological advances of the one are not lost in the exploration of the new human and emotional images of the other.

Debussy is the most fragile and introspective of these composers, lacking in broad and positive emotions. But his analysis of the harmonic problem broke ground for a new generation of musical thinkers. Sibelius, whose music has great strength and beauty, tended to limit himself nostalgically to the past of folklore and legend. Vaughan Williams throughout his career achieved most successfully the union of English folklore, and contemporary popular themes, to the symphonic tradition. Shostakovich is notable for the boisterous humor of his music, as in the last movement of his Sixth Symphony which resembles a New Orleans street march, and for such works as the Leningrad symphony, in which he makes the epic form as gripping as a four-act contemporary drama. Prokofiev has many lessons to teach in the adaptation of music to many different uses, with the greatest finesse, humor and tenderness, as in his concertos, his "Peter and the Wolf" and piano pieces for children, his music for the moving picture "Alexander Nevsky," his ballet "Romeo and Juliet," his stirring Fifth Symphony alive with memories of the past war. Such works in their handling of folk and popular material, are full of valuable lessons to the jazz composer.

Ives' folk material has a strong New England character, consisting of barn dances, street band music, hymn tunes, the songs that were sung during and after the Civil War. He is a most inventive composer in almost every form, such as song, chamber music and symphony.

His works have the remarkable character of being constructed with absolute classic soundness, and yet dealing
in the most ingratiating way with such specific programs
as American democratic history and traditions, Fourth of
July celebrations, Sunday picnics. It is that characteristic
of his which most baffles concert performers, his rhythmic
inventiveness leaping over bar lines and entering into
dazzling combinations, that should most interest the
jazzman, for many a jazz performance would look
equally baffling if written down on paper exactly as
played. A work of his that uses ragtime piano themes,
"A Night in Central Park," has a tonal rightness and
taste that puts to shame most attempts to write jazz of a
decade later.

Bartok is one of those composers using folk material
whose work represents a milepost in the history of music.
It is beautiful as music and an encyclopoedia of folk
style, analyzing the differences between the roots of folk
music and the sweetened dilutions of its language. His
compositions range from volumes of free settings of folk
songs for voice, piano and violin, to sonatas which exploit
the timbres and improvisational style of the folk musician, powerfully built concertos polyphonic in style, and
the deeply introspective string quartets, some of which
portray the anguish he felt at the first world war and
the rise of fascism. It is a revealing fact that the three
composers of our century who have had the most to teach
regarding the creative, contemporary use of folklore,

Vaughan Williams, Ives and Bartok, should have been among the least studied and publicized.

If it is plain that jazz composers have not begun to explore the technical possibilities they have before them, what are the possible musical forms in which jazz may be used? They may seem to be few, if we scan the average concert hall program. They are many, however, if we look at the whole art of music. Jazz is an art of song, and the history of music is full of composed song; some of it, like the songs of Purcell, Mozart, Schubert, Mussorgsky, Chaikowsky, very close in pattern and line to the folk and popular songs these composers knew. Jazz is an art of dance, and the composition of music in dance forms has an honored place in history from the suites of Bach, Handel and Rameau up through the ballet scores which are found in the work of almost every contemporary composer.

The symphony, while not a dance form, is not divorced from the dance. The symphonies of Haydn are full of dance patterns, not only in their minuets and brilliant finales, but often in the dramatic opening movements and tender slow movements. Dance patterns are found in the Beethoven symphonies, such as the Fourth, Sixth, Seventh and Eighth, as well as the symphonies of Schubert, Dvorak, Chaikowsky, Sibelius and many contemporary composers. The concerto is an interesting form for jazz composers to use, especially if they study the light-textured, improvisational form of the eighteenth century and earlier, instead of the more elaborate and heavy-handed romantic concerto.

Most important of all, because it takes in so many of the other musical forms, is opera. Opera is actually nothing more than a drama with music. The music may take on many different styles, from the symphonic fabric of Wagner and Berg, which is at the opposite pole from jazz, to the lighter textured song-speech and song form of Monteverdi, Purcell, Mozart, Verdi, and Mussorgsky, which has many parallels to jazz. So great a work as Mozart's "The Magic Flute" was, for example, almost a kind of popular vaudeville.

Thus jazz has almost limitless possibilities for use in larger forms of musical composition. The composition must be done, however, by men who both know the idiom itself thoroughly, and know the craft of composition. The failure of most composition up to now using jazz is due to the fact that the composers either did not know jazz, or that they did not know the various tools the history of music had fashioned, and the purposes of those tools, and so fell back upon the nearest, most pretentious platitudes.

What conditions are necessary for jazz to take this new and most important step?

One would be to raise musical instruction in the schools to a more intelligent level. The meaningless and destructive division between "classical" and "popular," born out of snobbery, should be thrown into the ashcan, like the practise of teaching students how to write the English language of today through a study of eighteenth century oratory.

The music schools, conservatories and music departments of the universities must undertake the task of analyzing and appraising the great modern composers and composing systems. They should undertake a systematic study of American music, particularly folk and jazz. There is no reason why young artists should study "tympani," for example, solely in terms of its use in a Berlioz symphony, when jazz has so many and new examples of the fine art of using the drums. Composers of the greatest talent should be encouraged to write songs for the American people, instead of leaving it to plagiarists and hacks.

Along with the growing, but painfully slow local sponsorship of symphony orchestras—left still too much to private philanthropy, with the accompanying snobbery and petty politics—there is no reason why each community should not sponsor a permanent large jazz band. A band can easily be put together of men capable of turning out a finished performance of Dixieland and New Orleans classics, of Ellington works, modern jazz jumps, and any new composition that comes along in jazz idiom. The one-sidedness and specialization that characterized jazz in the past has long broken down, and the modern jazz performer can enter with good taste into the styles of many periods of jazz.

The presence of such permanent organizations would remove much of the unwholesome atmosphere that now afflicts jazz; the exhausting travel, the one-night stands, the night club madness, the financial insecurity, the long hours, the unsettled home life. It would

encourage young composers to write for these bands, and to write a better music than the present "symphonic" jazz, a product of the mixture of movie palace and concert hall. Such bands could play for dances, break up into small New Orleans and jam session groups, give full-dress concerts, perform many different roles in the community life.

There is no doubt that such bands in one section of the country would sound different from those in another, which would be all to the good. They would take on the character of the regional folk art, so that the music of New Orleans, Kansas City, New York, Dallas, the far West and the Northwest would be revitalized. Our rich, wild folk lore, imperishable and yet now almost driven into the ground by the destructive centralization of Hollywood, radio and tin-pan-alley, would again have room to grow; and all refreshed by an interchange of ideas and musical creations from one center to another.

Lyric theatres could well be sponsored by communities. The sponsorship of local theatres, with music, would provide the ground on which a live operatic art could grow in America, one in which blues, jazz, all of American folk art would flower and take on contemporary themes, in which the art of creating honest music for the people could be brought back to life. The "bush leagues" could be recreated through which new talent could rise and stretch its wings.

Fundamental to all of these plans is the abolition of all forms of discrimination against minority peoples, as devastating to our music and cultural life as it is to our economic life and democracy. The achievements of jazz prove not only how deep rooted in people is the desire and ability to create, but how America has been robbed of the music of potentially great Negro composers, who never had a chance to produce the music of which they were capable. Nor does this loss involve only the Negro people. Jewish, Italian, Irish, and other peoples who came to these shores with a cultural heritage that could have added much to American life, were discouraged from using this heritage and instead given not a better culture, but the phony contrived and synthetic "popular" culture that is good business but bad art. They have nevertheless made a contribution. The creative gift of the Negro people to our popular music is of course paramount, but the Irish and Jewish song writers provided some of the best loved melodies of the past half century, in the days when, comparatively speaking, some genuine willingness to experiment existed in the music industry.

Comparing these projects with the present scene, they may seem Utopian. The commercial music networks are well entrenched, and any suggestions of music education, music organizations and community theatres sponsored by the government or by the people of a locality would be received in some quarters with outcries of horror.

Yet if the methods and principles of factory production of culture were all-conquering, both jazz and the art of musical composition in America would have long ago given up the ghost. Jazz players have fought for the right to create music as it pleased them to create, have gone hungry for it. This has meant the difference between manhood and serfdom, between the power of creation and the idiocy of mechanization.

Jazz shows the scars of this battle. It is often one-sided, narrow in its stock of emotions, suffering in isolation from its proper audiences, often embittered and de-

liberately shocking. But it is alive and creative. And it
has audiences, people who have tasted the pleasure of
music as it issues alive from men's minds and hands, and
will no longer accept a counterfeit. Other composers have
struggled to maintain the great traditions of the musical
art, to give America a music it apparently didn't want.
They too have suffered, but in a different way; from the
fact that concert and opera have become not a means to
bring composers and audiences together, but business
networks designed to offer for sale the cultural commodi-
ties of a past that have mellowed with time. The commercial music enterprises can never supply a living music
to America, whether "classical" or "popular," except by
chance, because they know only how to buy, revise, bor-
row and imitate the past, dressing it in eye-catching
clothing.

The task ahead is a difficult one, and the results will
be limited for a while to individual, local achievements;
the rise of a new and exciting jazz group, here and there,
or the emergence of a composer too powerful to shout
down or ignore; or the experiments of a ground-breaking
new music school; the formation in one locality or another of a people's sponsored cultural project. Most important of all will be the gathering strength of the struggle against jim-crow and all forms of discrimination, the
realization of how deeply this form of reaction eats into
our cultural life as well as into every other aspect of our
daily lives. A country doesn't exist apart from its people,

and an American musical life worthy of the name must be built on the music of its people, all of them. There can be no American national culture except as the result of the flowering of all the potential cultures of the peoples who together make up America. Music and the arts are too necessary to people to remain the monopoly of a mechanical system of production, subject to the whims of agents, managers, advertisers, publicists, book-keepers and investment bankers.

Jazz is the living embodiment of the creative powers of the people. It is especially the product, and gift to America, of the most poverty-stricken, hounded and exploited of the country, the Negro people. In it we can find the growing consciousness of the Negro people of their own solidarity as a people, a sense of national traditions, history and culture, born not out of Africa but out of their struggles against slavery, and out of the part they took in every struggle for the progress of American democracy from the War of Independence onward.

Jazz is the product of labor, in that the musician today is largely a kind of laborer. The free, creative and humanly expressive music that is hot jazz is the sign of the constant desire of the laborer to break out of the chains of mechanical production, to create a product that is worthy of him, one that bears the stamp of his mind and personality. Through the work of the musician it becomes the expression of the people from whom he comes and for whom he creates. Jazz holds within itself a precious emotional realism. Its content is of the life of those who are in the front line of the struggle to conquer nature, who work with hands and bodies, who live out every day of their lives the hardships and trials which every day brings up to all but a favored few. It is one of America's most precious cultural possessions, and its continued life is bound up with our life as a free people.

I N D E X

275